Creating a Space to

Is your outdoor area working? Do you want to make changes but are not sure where to start?

Creating a Space to Grow guides you through the process of changing and developing the outdoor environment of your early years setting to maximise the learning potential that these areas can offer. Packed full of strategies and ideas for enhancing outdoor areas, this new edition has been updated with references to the revised Early Years Foundation Stage and features many new colour photographs to illustrate how different settings have enhanced their outside spaces.

Aimed at all early years practitioners who are looking to fulfil the potential learning opportunities that a stimulating outdoor area can create, this key text includes:

- practical 'real life' case studies and examples from the Kent 'Space to Grow' project;
- step-by-step photocopiable prompt sheets that guide you through each stage and encourage the participation of your children;
- a new section that includes updates from some of the Kent settings and new guidance on auditing and improving your outdoor space.

Focusing on the core values that highlight the importance and benefits of outdoor play, this essential book will enable you to recognise the true value that outdoor spaces can have on a child's overall development and well-being.

Gail Ryder Richardson is an independent trainer and consultant with thirty years' experience in the early years sector. Her consultancy service *Outdoor Matters!* offers information and support to the early years sector through advisory visits, training, conferences and projects.

Learning through Landscapes (LTL) is the national school grounds charity, campaigning for positive outdoor learning and play experiences for all children in education and child care.

Also available:

Learning Outdoors
Improving the Quality of Young Children's Play Outdoors
Edited by Helen Bilton
ISBN 978-1-84312-350-7

Playing Outside
Activities, Ideas and Inspiration for the Early Years
Helen Bilton
ISBN 978-1-84312-067-4

Outdoor Learning in the Early Years (Third Edition)
Management and Innovation
Helen Bilton
ISBN 978-0-415-45477-3

Organising Play in the Early Years
Practical Ideas for Teachers and Assistants
Jane Drake
ISBN 978-1-84312-025-4

Planning for Children's Play and Learning (Third Edition)
Meeting Children's Needs in the Later Stages of the EYFS
Jane Drake
ISBN 978-0-415-48597-5

The Early Years Curriculum
A View from Outdoors
Gloria Callaway
ISBN 978-1-84312-345-3

Creating a Space to Grow

Developing your enabling environment outdoors

Second edition

Gail Ryder Richardson

Routledge
Taylor & Francis Group

LONDON AND NEW YORK

Second edition published 2014
by Routledge
2 Park Square, Milton Park, Abingdon, Oxon OX14 4RN

Simultaneously published in the USA and Canada
by Routledge
711 Third Avenue, New York, NY 10017

Routledge is an imprint of the Taylor & Francis Group, an informa business

First edition published 2006 by David Fulton Publishers
Reprinted 2010 by Routledge

British Library Cataloguing in Publication Data
A catalogue record for this book is available from the British Library

Library of Congress Cataloging in Publication Data
Richardson, Gail Ryder.
Creating a space to grow : developing your enabling environment outdoors / Gail Ryder Richardson. –
2nd edition.
pages cm
ISBN 978-0-415-82555-9 (pbk.) – ISBN 978-0-203-75848-9 (ebook) 1. Outdoor education. I. Title.
LB1047.R48 2013
371.3'84–dc23
2012051251

ISBN: 978-0-415-82555-9 (pbk)
ISBN: 978-0-203-75848-9 (ebk)

Typeset in Bembo
by FiSH Books Ltd, Enfield

Printed and bound in India by Replika Press Pvt. Ltd.

Contents

Foreword

This book solves problems! Gail Ryder Richardson has successfully addressed the issue of the obstacles that stop babies and young children having access to the outdoor learning environment, and shown how these can be overcome. This is achieved not in the abstract but in step-by-step prompts and guidelines, based on real case studies. Practitioners can read about many situations – for example where settings have to share spaces with other groups or have only limited space for free-flow play – and can be inspired to make a start on developing their own area. Follow or adapt the prompt sheets to your own situation and it all seems possible.

Two things are essential if young children are to have free access to an outside learning environment of quality. The first, of course, is space, directly leading to and from the indoor play room. The second prerequisite to worthwhile outdoor play is the knowledgeable and enthusiastic practitioner. This is the book to ignite that enthusiasm into action and deepen the knowledge of how to offer children the best environment for learning and the space to grow.

Marjorie Ouvry
Author of *Exercising Muscles and Minds: Outdoor Play and the Early Years Curriculum*

Gail Ryder Richardson – *Outdoor Matters!*

Gail has worked for 30 years in a wide range of roles within the early years sector including advice and support, education inspections and quality assurance. From January 2008 until March 2011 she worked for the National Strategies to support and challenge local authorities across the South East to improve educational outcomes for children under five years old. Prior to this, Gail was a Senior Development Officer for Learning through Landscapes. In this role she delivered the Space to Grow project and provided early years advice and expertise to local authorities, schools and settings. She contributed to the development of the Outdoor Play Vision and Value statements, and the in-depth guidance for the Enabling Environment theme within the *Early Years Foundation Stage* (2007).

Gail now works as an independent trainer and consultant. Her consultancy service *Outdoor Matters!* offers information and support to the early years sector through advisory visits, training, conferences and projects. For more information, please visit www.outdoormatters.co.uk.

Learning through Landscapes (LTL)

Learning through Landscapes is the UK charity dedicated to enhancing outdoor learning and play for children. Our vision is that every child benefits from stimulating outdoor learning and play in their education. We aim to enable children to connect with nature, be more active, be more engaged with their learning, develop their social skills and have fun!

We do this through three avenues:

- advocating the benefits of outdoor learning and play at school and preschool;
- inspiring and enabling the design and development of outdoor environments to support children's development;
- inspiring and enabling teachers and early years practitioners to develop the confidence, ideas and skills they need to make better use of outdoor spaces.

We are the only UK charity specialising in outdoor learning and play in education. Our unrivalled knowledge and expertise is based on more than twenty years' experience of practical action and research.

www.ltl.org.uk

Learning
through
Landscapes

Space to Grow

The Kent Space to Grow project was a collaborative venture between Learning through Landscapes and Kent Early Years Development and Childcare Partnership (EYDCP) to address concerns about the quality of outdoor play within early years settings across Kent.

The aim of the project was to provide real examples of good practice, thus inspiring and motivating all settings in the county to develop their outdoor play provision. An inspirational publication based on case study material collected during the project, rather than a final report, was identified as an important output of the programme. *Creating a Space to Grow* has enabled the findings and achievements of the project to be disseminated widely, thus being of benefit to early years practitioners in Kent and beyond.

The twenty-two settings involved in the project are listed below:

Bedgebury Junior School – Foundation Stage Unit, Goudhurst
Bell Wood Community Primary School, Maidstone
Bertie's Playgroup, Faversham
Bright Beginnings Day Nursery, Dartford
Ditton Church Preschool, Ditton
Glebe House Day Nursery, Larkfield
Happy Faces Preschool, Tonbridge
Highways at Hamstreet Kindergarten, Hamstreet
Little Acorns (Herne) Preschool, Herne
Mary Sheridan Preschool, Canterbury
MCNA Preschool, Margate
Mongeham Primary School – Foundation Stage Unit, Mongeham
Northfleet Nursery School, Northfleet
Pipsqueaks Day Nursery, Queensborough
Saplings@The Sports Centre, Tunbridge Wells
St John's Primary School and Preschool, Sevenoaks
St Martin's Preschool, Folkestone
St Martin's Preschool Group, Dover
Sticky Fingers Day Nursery, Ramsgate
Sunshine and Showers Nursery School, St Mary's Bay
Victoria Road Primary School, Ashford
White Oak Preschool, Swanley

Acknowledgements

My sincere gratitude and appreciation goes to all those people who supported and encouraged me, first in the delivery of the Kent Space to Grow project and second throughout the writing of this book. In particular I would like to acknowledge the involvement of the following people.

Jan White, LTL's Senior Early Years Development Officer, and Jenny Middleton (formerly Kent's Senior Early Years Advisory Teacher) who worked together to develop the initial ideas for an outdoor project in Kent.

Peter Carne, Director of Operations at LTL, for his unshakeable confidence in my ability to deliver the project and write this book.

Alison Clark from the Thomas Coram Research Unit, for her inspiration and encouragement.

Julia, Chris, Zoë, Steve, Jake and 'lovely Jenny' – the 'LTL in London' team who shared in the laughter and the tears – a big thank you to you all!

The Kent Early Years Advisory Team, particularly Julia Gouldson, Training and Quality Manager, and Karen Rolls, Senior Early Years Advisory Teacher.

And lastly, but most importantly, the children, parents, staff and management at all twenty-two Kent settings involved in the project and featured in this book – it couldn't have been written without you!

Introduction

Ten years ago an innovative collaboration between Kent Early Years and Childcare Partnership (EYDCP), and Learning through Landscapes (LTL), a well-respected national charity, resulted in the first edition of this book. Written for LTL, as a testimony to the success of the Space to Grow project, the book charted the journey made by practitioners in Kent as they sought to develop and improve their use of the outdoor environment for children's play learning and development. The developments and improvements within the project focused on increasing children's access to outdoors, improving the quality of their play and learning experiences, and overcoming lower levels of confidence and enthusiasm for outdoor learning amongst early years practitioners. The processes of improving practice, overcoming challenges and identifying solutions have stood the test of time and remain relevant to practitioners today. However, other aspects of the first edition, such as the curriculum references, have been superseded and are now less useful.

This second edition of *Creating a Space to Grow* aims to inspire the next generation of early years practitioners. Obsolete material has been revised to ensure that the content and curriculum references are helpful to today's practitioners wishing to develop their own outdoor environment. Chapter 1 identifies the special nature of the outdoor environment, delivery of the curriculum outdoors and the implications for practitioners and their role as outdoor educators. Chapters 2–5 focus on the original processes of the project in order to preserve the integrity of the book as an outcome of the project. In these chapters the LTL approach to changing and developing the outdoor environment is described in detail, and the case studies demonstrate how the Kent settings identified and overcame a range of issues that hamper the provision of good outdoor play. Finally, in Chapter 6 there is new material that includes updates from the eight of the settings originally involved in the project and an outline of the *Outdoor Matters!* approach to managing change and improving practice. I have enjoyed revisiting the project settings and am delighted that the project inspired practitioners to make improvements that have stood the test of time and have improved the quality of outdoor provision for children. The Kent settings continue to reflect on their practice and I hope this book will encourage you to evaluate and make changes to your own outdoor practice.

The Space to Grow project

In September 2003, Learning through Landscapes worked with twenty-two early years settings in Kent. The settings include community preschools, reception classes, an independent school, private preschools and day nurseries, as well as preschools funded by other bodies such as social services and health authorities. Some settings had reasonable access to a safe secure outdoor environment and some had little or no outdoor space of their own.

The original aim of Kent's Early Years Development and Childcare Partnership (EYDCP) was to help maintained and non-maintained early years settings to improve their outdoor play provision and practice. The Space to Grow project was funded by Kent EYDCP to develop demonstration settings in Kent across the range of early years provision. The settings involved were supported to identify their own barriers to offering effective outdoor learning, and to develop a range of relevant, copiable low-tech and affordable solutions, that other early years providers could realistically transfer to their own situations. All the settings involved in the project made a commitment to provide access and share their practice with other settings, to inspire and motivate them to enhance their own provision.

The wider intentions of the project were:

- to aid early years settings to move forwards in their provision and practice for outdoor play towards an integrated indoor-outdoor experience for children;
- to help settings in Kent meet the National Standards for Day Care and Childminding, the *Birth to Three Matters Framework*, the Foundation Stage curriculum requirements and the Kent Quality Kitemark;
- to find appropriate solutions to the limitations and barriers that prevent children from accessing and using the outdoors to its full potential;
- to identify and develop management strategies for achieving high-quality outdoor provision;
- to contribute to the development and dissemination of sound pedagogy for outdoor play in the early years;
- to create demonstration sites in a range of settings to which all settings could relate, exploring the factors specific to different kinds of provision (e.g. preschools, private nurseries, nursery and reception provision in schools) and disseminating good practice, enthusiasm and confidence;
- to create and encourage a network of support and communication throughout the Kent Early Years sector;
- to map out the process of change regarding outdoor provision in a wide range of settings, developing the process to make best use of the potential for children's well-being and development, family involvement and staff team effectiveness, to provide a model for change adoptable by others at the beginning of their journey.

Learning through Landscapes supported each setting through a process of change and development using participative approaches that engaged the whole setting community – in particular the children – at each stage of the process of developing their outdoor area.

This second edition still includes all the techniques that were used in Kent. Consultation with, and the involvement of, children is more likely to be successful if it is already embedded in the working practices of the setting. However, there are ideas for each stage of the process to enable practitioners to involve children in 'Getting started', 'Thinking and planning', 'Making it happen' and 'Evaluating and enjoying'. Each idea has been written up as a prompt sheet that identifies:

- when to use the activity;
- preparation and resources;
- how to gather the information;
- how to make sense of the information;
- other issues to consider.

The Kent Space to Grow project also provided an invaluable opportunity for working collaboratively with Alison Clark, at that time a research officer at the Thomas Coram Research Unit of the Institute of Education, University of London. Alison Clark carried out a pilot research project 'Spaces to Play' in Happy Faces Preschool, one of the project settings in Kent. The research focused on using and extending the tools developed as part of the 'Mosaic approach' to explore young children's understanding and use of their outdoor play space. The resulting publication *Spaces to Play: More Listening to Young Children Using the Mosaic Approach* by Alison Clark and Peter Moss explored how to listen to young children's views and experiences of their outdoor environment, in order to inform change. It described the adaptation of the Mosaic approach to work with young children in outdoor spaces and demonstrates young children's competence in expressing their opinions on their environment. It discussed the challenges and future directions for practitioners and researchers in listening to young children.

All the Kent settings involved in the project recognised the importance of improving children's opportunities for outdoor learning and the staff teams worked hard to identify their priorities, and find ways of overcoming the limitations of their own outdoor space.

Although Learning through Landscapes' direct involvement with the original twenty-two Kent settings finished in 2005 the work of the project continues to this day.

Alison Clark working with children at Happy Faces Preschool

1 Why do children need to be outdoors?

The special nature of outdoors

The outdoor environment has features that are either different from indoors or cannot be offered on the same scale, or in the same way, indoors. Early years practitioners who recognise the special nature of outdoors acknowledge that it provides a significantly different and complementary environment for nurturing children's well-being and supporting their learning. Learning through Landscapes identifies nine features that contribute to the special nature of outdoors as a learning and play environment for children.

Freedom

The outdoors offers children many freedoms, which may extend or be different from the freedoms they can experience indoors.

- Freedom to move around in a bigger space – vigorous activity, larger-scale play, or just 'feel' the space around them.
- Freedom to be more relaxed and inventive about exploring and using materials and resources – transporting, mixing, making a mess.
- Freedom to be boisterous and to make noise without disrupting others.
- Freedom to explore different ways of being, feeling, behaving and interacting – from active super-hero play to cloud watching.

Space

Outdoors offers children additional space, upwards as well as sideways. The children can be at different levels, see things from a range of perspectives and have the sky as their 'roof'.

- Outdoor space feels very different from indoors and includes light effects, air movements and temperature changes.
- Outdoors offers added space that encourages children to be more active and work on a larger scale across all areas of learning, and supports collaborative activity.
- Outdoors offers children a different mental and emotional space from that which exists indoors – it just *feels* different!

Contact with the natural world

- The outdoors offers children direct, extended and deeply engaging experiences with plants, mini-beasts, other animals such as birds, soil, sand and many other natural materials. The four 'elements' of earth, air, water and even fire (through outdoor cooking or role-play barbeques) need to be experienced directly.

Whole-body, multi-sensory experiences

- Young children use their body to learn, by moving, doing and using all their senses. All babies and young children, and particularly those with sensory impairments, benefit from a multi-sensory environment.
- Children can be vigorous, boisterous and active for long periods. They can use their upper body and limbs, developing health, strength and co-ordination and enjoying and learning about what their bodies can do.

Real experiences

● Real and direct experiences are easily offered outdoors through growing, experimenting with natural materials such as sand (on a large scale), running water and elements of the weather – rain, snow, frost, sunshine and so on. The sounds and sights of the locality and community can be experienced then explored through outdoor play, especially in pretend and role-play. Children can gain real understanding of concepts such as volume and weight when transporting a barrow-full of sand, and distance or height when using the physical play apparatus.

Variety of spaces, places and perspectives

- In addition to open space, outdoors can offer nooks and crannies among plants, climbing frames, playhouses and dens. Children can be enclosed (under or inside) or high up with a new perspective of looking down on their world.
- Spaces can be active and provide large-scale opportunities, or can be places for calm, reflection, one-to-one interaction or the chance to be by oneself.
- Spaces can be soft or hard or anything in between, giving a range of sensations through surfaces and planting.

Dynamic experiences

- Outdoors offers children the freedom to manipulate, change and be in control of their environment. Through the use of moveable, open-ended resources and materials, they can create new play environments. The daily changes in the quality of the air, temperature and rainfall and the gradual changes through the seasons offer huge potential for real and direct experience and exploration – every day is different! The uncertainty of daily changes and the surprise and excitement arising from spontaneous events, such as finding a ladybird or spotting a hot air balloon overhead, are all waiting to be captured and used to enrich children's experiences as they find out about their world.

Relaxed relationships with adults and other children

There is a different quality to the relationships a child can have outside with other children and with adults.

- Children can choose to interact on a variety of activity levels or group sizes.
- Working on a large scale or with bikes with trailers provides opportunities to co-operate, negotiate and collaborate.
- Adults can take time to sit and chat, get involved in play and exploration or simply stand back to observe and listen to children's play. Many adults find they are happy to tolerate higher levels of noise, mess and activity in the bigger, unrestricted space with no ceiling and have less concern about spillages or collision with obstacles.

- Children respond differently to adults outside. For example, some children who talk little inside are less inhibited outdoors. It is often possible to engage children in activities outdoors that they are reluctant to participate in inside, for example mark-making or counting.

Challenges and risky experiences

- Outdoors provides experiences through which children can learn how to keep themselves safe and how to be aware of the safety of others.
- It offers children many ways to be adventurous and to challenge their own limits within a framework of safety provided by adults and the environment they have prepared.

A shared vision and core values for outdoor play

In Kent, all early years settings within the county have support from early years advisors. Through their ongoing contact with providers, Kent's early years advisory team had identified that some settings were having difficulties in providing children with good access to a stimulating outdoor environment and support from enthusiastic adults. The creation of the Space to Grow project was the first step towards addressing this concern. However, in order to develop and endorse a shared vision of what good outdoor play should look like the Kent early years team also formed a partnership with other leading early years organisations and consultants with professional interests in outdoor play. Led by the national school grounds charity, Learning through Landscapes, the Vision and Values Partnership brought together leading thinkers, pedagogues and organisations from across the early years sector. (See pages 14–15 for a list of those involved in this process.)

The Vision and Values Partnership worked to create a set of statements that would exemplify the importance they placed on offering young children the opportunities to learn and play outdoors, to connect with the natural world and to use outdoors as a context for developing strong relationships with adults and other children.

These statements were first published by *Nursery World* magazine in 2004 and were subsequently included in the support materials for the Early Years Foundation Stage (2007). Following some amendments and additions in 2008, the document continues to underpin expectations for outdoor play within the EYFS (2012).

Outdoor play – the shared vision for all young children

- All children have the right to experience and enjoy the essential and special nature of being outdoors. Young children thrive and their minds and bodies develop best when they have free access to stimulating outdoor environments for learning through play and real experiences. Knowledgeable and enthusiastic adults are crucial to unlocking the potential of outdoors.

Core values for high-quality outdoor experiences for young children

1 Young children should be outdoors as much as indoors and need a well-designed, well-organised, integrated indoor–outdoor environment, preferably with indoors and outdoors available simultaneously.

Outdoor provision is an essential part of the child's daily environment and life, not an option or an extra. Each half of the indoor–outdoor environment offers significantly different, but complementary, experiences and ways of being to young children. They should be available simultaneously and be experienced in a joined-up way, with each being given equal status and attention for their contribution to young children's well-being, health and stimulation and all areas of development. Outdoor space must be considered a necessary part of an early years environment and be well thought through and well organised to maximise its value and

usability by children and adults. Design and planning must support developmentally appropriate practice, being driven by children's interests and needs.

2   Play is the most important activity for young children outside.

Play is the means through which children find stimulation, well-being and happiness, and is the means through which they grow physically, intellectually and emotionally. Play is the most important thing for children to do outside and the most relevant way of offering learning outdoors. The outdoor environment is very well suited to meeting children's needs for all types of play, building upon first-hand experiences.

3   Outdoor provision can, and must, offer young children experiences that have a lot of meaning to them and are led by the child.

Because of the freedom the outdoors offers to move on a large scale, to be active, noisy and messy and to use all their senses with their whole body, young children engage in the way they most need to explore, make sense of life and express their feeling and ideas. Many young children relate much more strongly to learning offered outdoors rather than indoors.
    All areas of learning must be offered through a wide range of holistic experiences, both active and calm, which make the most of what the outdoors has to offer.
    Outdoor provision needs to be organised so that children are stimulated, and able, to follow their own interests and needs through play-based activity, giving them independence, self-organisation, participation and empowerment. The adult role is crucial in achieving this effectively.

4   Young children need all the adults around them to understand why outdoor play provision is essential for them, and they need adults who are committed and able to make its potential available to them.

Young children need practitioners who value and enjoy the outdoors themselves, see the potential and consequences it has for young children's well-being and development, and want to be outside with them. Attitude, understanding, commitment and positive thinking are important, as well as the skills to make the best use of what the outdoors has to offer and to effectively support child-led learning; the adult role outdoors must be as deeply considered as that indoors. Practitioners must be able to recognise, capture and share children's learning outdoors with parents and other people working with the child, so that they too become enthused. Cultural differences in attitude to the outdoors need to be understood and worked with sensitively to reach the best outcomes for children.

5   The outdoor space and curriculum must harness the special nature of the outdoors, to offer children what the indoors cannot. This should be the focus for outdoor provision, complementing and extending provision indoors.

The outdoors offers young children essential experiences vital to their well-being, health and development in all areas. Children who miss these experiences are significantly deprived. Outdoors, children can have the freedom to explore different ways of 'being', feeling, behaving and interacting; they have space – physical (upwards as well as sideways), mental and emotional; they have room and permission to be active, interactive, messy, noisy and work on a large scale; they may feel less controlled by adults.

The real contact with the elements, the seasons and the natural world, the range of perspectives, sensations and environments – multi-dimensional and multi-sensory – and the daily change, uncertainty, surprise and excitement all contribute to the desire young children have to be outside. It cannot be the same indoors, a child cannot be the same indoors – outdoors is a vital, special and deeply engaging place for young children.

6   Outdoors should be a dynamic, flexible and versatile place where children can choose, create, change and be in charge of their play environment.

Outdoor provision can, and should, offer young children an endlessly versatile, changeable and responsive environment for all types of play where they can manipulate, create, control and modify. This offers a huge sense of freedom, which is not readily available indoors. It also underpins the development of creativity and the dispositions for learning. The space itself and the resources, layout, planning and routines all need to be versatile, open-ended and flexible to maximise their value to the child.

7   Young children must have a rich outdoor environment full of irresistible stimuli, contexts for play, exploration and talk, and plenty of real experiences and contact with the natural world and with the community.

Through outdoor play, young children can learn the skills of social interaction and friendship, care for living things and their environment, be curious and fascinated, experience awe, wonder and joy and become 'lost in the experience'. They can satisfy their deep urge to explore,

experiment and understand and become aware of their community and locality, thus developing a sense of connection to the physical, natural and human worlds. A particular strength of outdoor provision is that it offers children many opportunities to experience the real world, have first-hand experiences, do real tasks and do what adults do, including being involved in the care of the outdoor space. Settings should make the most of this aspect, with connected play opportunities.

An aesthetic awareness of, and emotional link to, the non-constructed or controlled, multi-sensory and multi-dimensional natural world is a crucial component of human well-being, and increasingly absent in young children's lives. The richness of cultural diversity is an important part of our everyday world; this can and should be explored by children through outdoor experiences. Giving children a sense of belonging to something bigger than the immediate family or setting lays foundations for living as a community.

Young children should have long periods of time outside. They need to know that they can be outside every day when they want to, and that they can develop their ideas for play over time. High-quality play outdoors, where children are deeply involved, only emerges when they know they are not hurried. They need to have time to develop their use of spaces and resources and uninterrupted time to develop their play ideas, or to construct a place and then play in it or to get into problem-solving on a big scale. They need to be able to return to projects again and again until 'finished' with them.

Slow learning is good learning, giving time for assimilation. When children can move between indoors and outside, their play or explorations develop further still. Young children also need time (and places) to daydream, look on or simply relax outside.

8   Young children need challenge and risk within a framework of security and safety. The outdoor environment lends itself to offering challenge, helping children learn how to be safe and to be aware of others.

Children are seriously disadvantaged if they do not learn how to approach and manage physical and emotional risk. They can become either timid or reckless, or be unable to cope with consequences. Young children need to be able to set and meet their own challenges, become aware of their limits and push their abilities (at their own pace), be prepared to make mistakes, and experience the pleasure of feeling capable and competent. Challenge and its associated risk are vital for this. Young children also need to learn how to recognise and manage risk as life-skills, so as to become able to act safely, for themselves and others.

Safety of young children outdoors is paramount and a culture of 'risk assessment to enable' that permeates every aspect of outdoor provision is vital for all settings. Young children also need to feel secure, nurtured and valued outdoors. This includes clear behavioural boundaries (using rules to enable freedom), nurturing places and times outside, and respect for how individual children prefer to play and learn.

9   Outdoor provision must support inclusion and meet the needs of individuals, offering a diverse range of play-based experiences.

Provision for learning outdoors is responsive to the needs of very active learners, those who need sensory or language stimulation and those who need space away from others – it makes provision more inclusive and is a vital learning environment. When children's learning styles are valued, their self-image benefits. Boys, who tend to use active learning modes more than girls and until they are older, are particularly disadvantaged by limited outdoor play.

All children need full access to provision outdoors and it is important to know and meet the needs and interests of each child as an individual. Young children react differently to the spaces and experiences available or created, so awareness and flexibility are key to the adult role. Observation and assessment (both formative and summative), and intervention for particular support, must be carried out outside. While it is important to ensure the safety of all children, it is equally important to ensure that all are sufficiently challenged.

10 Young children should participate in decisions and actions affecting their outdoor play.

Young children should take an active part in decisions and actions for outdoor provision, big and small. Their perspectives and views are critical and must be sought, and they can take an active role in setting up, clearing away and caring for the outdoor space.

The Vision and Values for Outdoor Play have been developed and endorsed by the following individuals and organisations:

Bexley Council
Diane Rich, Rich Learning Opportunities
Early Childhood Forum
Early Education
Early Excellence
Education Walsall
ESIS (Wales)

ESTYN (HMI Education and Training in Wales)
Forum for Maintained Nursery Schools
Grounds for Learning
Helen Bilton, author and consultant
Integrated Inspection Scotland
Kent County Council
Learning through Landscapes
Margaret Edgington, author and consultant
Marjorie Ouvry, author and consultant
Mindstretchers
National Day Nurseries Association
Neath Port Talbot Council
Nursery World magazine
Paddy Beels, Wingate Family Centre
Pre-school Learning Alliance
Sightlines Initiative
Stirling Council
Sue Humphries, author and consultant
Thomas Coram Institute
Welsh Assembly Government (was the National Assembly)
West Sussex County Council

In 2008, the following organisations and individuals joined the Partnership to refine the statements and agree collaborative ways to work together to promote the importance of outdoor learning and play.

Angela Anning, author, consultant, academic
Asquith Day Nurseries
Gail Ryder Richardson, *Outdoor Matters!*
Helen Tovey, academic and author
Jan White, author and consultant
Jenny Doyle, Forest Schools
Julian Grenier, academic and consultant
Peter Carne OBE
Play England
Surrey County Council
The Council for Learning Outside the Classroom
Trio Childcare Connections

The curriculum outdoors

Very young children have a fascination with natural outdoor environments and yet many have very few opportunities to experience outdoor play. A 2009 report to Natural England on Childhood and Nature observed that 'Children spend less time playing in natural places, such as woodlands, countryside and heaths; less than 10% play in the natural places compared to 40% of their parents and grandparents when they were young' (p. 8). The provision of good quality outdoor experiences in early years settings is particularly important since it is one of the few natural environments in which today's children have regular play opportunities.

Ten years ago, when the Space to Grow project was being delivered, early years settings were implementing the *Birth to Three Matters Framework* and the *Curriculum Guidance for the Foundation*

Stage. Practitioners working within these frameworks were required to acknowledge and respond to the explicit expectation that good quality learning experiences would be provided outdoors as well as indoors, for both babies and young children.

However, in the intervening decade the early years curriculum has undergone several transformations. In 2008 the *Birth to Three Matters Framework* and the *Curriculum Guidance for the Foundation Stage* were replaced by the original EYFS (2007). This document provided practitioners with a single statutory framework and non-statutory guidance covering the first five years of a child's life and it placed high importance on the use of the outdoor environment:

> Wherever possible, there should be access to an outdoor play area, and this is the expected norm for providers. In provision where outdoor play space cannot be provided, outings should be planned and taken on a daily basis.
>
> (EYFS (2007) Statutory Framework, p. 35)

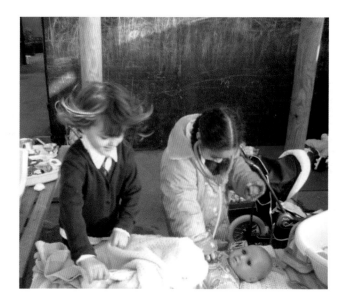

In 2011, the Tickell Review considered the impact of the EYFS (2007) on children's outcomes, and on those working in the early years. The review, *Early Years; Foundations for life Health and Learning*, consulted widely within the sector and sought to 'build on what was working well in the existing EYFS framework, and improve those areas that are causing problems' (p. 2).

The report on the *Evidence for the Early Years Foundation Stage (EYFS) Review* identified that 'There is widespread support for the role of outdoor activities in supporting children's development' (p. 22). Comments made as part of the consultation confirmed that practitioners and parents recognised and valued the impact that outdoors has on children's learning and well-being:

'If we are looking to help children achieve economic well-being then we need to be giving children more opportunities to be outside.'

Nursery practitioner

'As for my child's health, I LOVE the fact that outdoor play has taken on such a major role in the new reception life.'

Parent

The Early Years Foundation Stage (EYFS) Review – Report on the Evidence p. 22

In England, the revised EYFS (2012) framework continues to include emphasis on the importance of the outdoor environment: 'Providers must provide access to an outdoor play area or, if that is not possible, ensure that outdoor activities are planned and taken on a daily basis' (p. 24), and the revised guidance, *Development Matters in the Early Years Foundation Stage*, is full of helpful examples of outdoor practice. The last decade has seen the curriculum evolving in other parts of the UK, and the early years frameworks in place across Scotland and Wales also promote the use of outdoors. In Scotland the curriculum document notes:

> Well-constructed and well-planned outdoor learning helps develop the skills of enquiry, critical thinking and reflection necessary for our children and young people to meet the social, economic and environmental challenges of life in the 21st century. Outdoor learning connects children and young people with the natural world, with our built heritage and our culture and society, and encourages lifelong involvement and activity in Scotland's outdoors.
>
> (*Curriculum for Excellence through Outdoor Learning*, p. 7)

In Wales the curriculum document states that 'the Foundation Phase environment should promote discovery and independence and a greater emphasis on using the outdoor environment as a resource for children's learning' (p. 4). Whilst Northern Ireland has a long-established rationale for using outdoors:

> The outdoor area provides young children with one of the best possible environments in which to learn. Any adult who has watched children playing in a well planned and well resourced outdoor area with involved adults will have observed the joy and excitement they experience as they learn new skills and make fresh discoveries.
>
> (*Learning Outdoors in the Early Years: A Resource Book*)

The practitioners involved in the Space to Grow project were implementing the English curriculum and this second edition will also focus on how the outdoors supports delivery of the EYFS (2012). However, practitioners working in other parts of the UK, or other parts of the world will recognise how the key elements of good outdoor practice can be transposed and embedded within their own curriculum.

So, how does the special nature of the outdoor environment support and enrich curriculum experiences for babies and toddlers?

The EYFS (2012) guidance states that 'children develop in the context of relationships and the environment around them' it goes on to recognise that 'the ways in which a child engages with other people and their environment . . . underpin learning and development across all areas and support the child to remain an effective and motivated learner' (p. 4). A motivated and effective learner is a child who uses all their senses to find out about whatever they come into contact with, including people, toys, clothes, books, flowers, grass and anything else. Their curiosity leads them to understand that some things are predictable while others are not. Children who are effective learners watch the things that go on around them and they often imitate what they see and hear. They use materials imaginatively and creatively and begin to represent their ideas using marks. They are also investigators and explorers who try to find out how things work, and who create new uses for things. They are very active learners both physically, using their bodies, and mentally, using their minds.

Outdoors provides a place:

- where babies and toddlers become able to trust and rely on their own abilities, find out and become confident and competent in what they can do, valuing and appreciating their own abilities; where babies and toddlers can become sociable and effective communicators using their developing physical skills to make social contact, encouraging conversation, learning new words and meanings, describing, questioning and predicting; in which babies and toddlers can explore, experiment, play and respond to the world creatively and imaginatively and make connections through the senses and movement to find out about the environment and other people; where children can be active, acquire physical skills and gain control of their bodies, make decisions and choices and become aware of others and their needs.

Outdoors provides a place where practitioners can:

- support babies and toddlers, to enable them to gain confidence and to encourage them try new things; find time to play, sing and laugh with young babies;
- create areas in which toddlers can sit and chat with friends or with staff, for example in a cosy outdoor den; be available to explore and talk about things that interest young babies and toddlers outdoors, and listen and respond to their questions, both serious and playful; thoroughly investigate the environment with children; for example, when outside consider how to shift leaves off a path, enlarge or 'disappear' a puddle, collect water dripping from a tap; provide opportunities for creative, physical outdoor experiences for babies such as bouncing, rolling and splashing.

The outdoor environment offers endless stimuli to interest babies and toddlers, and a huge variety of materials and resources to feed their strong urge to explore and discover. The outdoors provides wonderful experiences to support the development of the child as a competent learner. It is important that they have plenty of time outdoors every day, and essential that they can share their curiosity and delight with a playful, interested, observant and attentive adult.

So, how does the special nature of the outdoor environment support and enrich curriculum experiences for children over three years old?

Children need purposeful and engaging experiences outdoors that help them to develop in several areas of the curriculum at the same time in a natural way that draws on their own styles of behaving and learning. Outdoors is a place that supports progress towards early learning goals within all areas of learning. It offers children countless different experiences and, in many cases, these experiences are better when they take place outdoors, or sometimes only possible at all in an outdoor environment.

The EYFS (2007) identified that provision for learning outdoors should give children meaningful opportunities to:

run, climb, pedal, throw...

- be physical on a large and a small scale
- enjoy a wide range of playful physical experiences
- take pleasure in movement and enjoy their bodies

be excited, energetic, adventurous, noisy...

- be energetic and boisterous
- be adventurous, with ideas as well as physically
- be uninhibited about being noisy and messy

talk, interact, make friends...

- use language to communicate and socialise
- explore ideas and have fun together
- play together, collaborate and co-operate

imagine, dream, invent...

- listen to, tell and act out stories
- engage in many kinds of pretend, fantasy and role-play
- explore behaving differently and 'being' someone else

create, construct...

- be imaginative, creative and expressive
- be inventive, constructive, de-constructive and find out how things work
- play in their own constructions and develop them

investigate, explore, discover, experiment...

- be curious and be fascinated
- experience and explore all kinds of materials and phenomena
- try out ideas and theories about how things behave or work

make music, express...

- make sounds and music with a range of items
- dance, chant rhymes and sing
- listen to and be influenced by a range of music
- express ideas, thoughts and feelings through a range of media using the scale and inspiration of the outdoors

find patterns, experience meanings...

- represent, make marks and see the written word
- experience and explore mathematical ideas and thinking
- have real experiences in order to really understand concepts

dig, grow, nurture...

- dig in sand, soil and mud
- grow a range of plants and witness growth, change and the seasonal cycles
- care for and nurture plants, wildlife and kept animals

hide, relax, find calm, reflect...

- be comfortable, calm, dream and enjoy being alone
- explore who they are and how they belong
- be themselves and play in their own way, at their own pace

have responsibility, be independent, collaborate...

- manage their own play and work together
- play and work with adults as equals
- change their play environment through flexible, versatile resources.

Outdoors and the Early Years Foundation Stage (2012)

The EYFS (2012) re-emphasises some important aspects of the original document in order to strengthen practice and improve outcomes for children. It asserts that there are characteristics that 'underpin learning and development across all areas' and that these characteristics – playing and exploring, active learning and creating and thinking critically – 'support the child to remain an effective and motivated learner' (*Development Matters in the EYFS* 2012, p. 4) The revised framework also acknowledges that some areas of learning are of particular importance to very young children since they provide the underpinning foundation for successful lifelong learning. Within the revised documentation these 'prime areas' are identified as: personal, social and emotional development; communication and language; and physical development. The remaining four areas of learning identified as 'specific areas' include 'essential skills and knowledge that children need to participate successfully in society' and have been identified as literacy, mathematics, understanding of the world and expressive arts and design.

In 2007, *Effective Practice Outdoor Learning*, the in-depth guidance for the original EYFS, recognised that the effective use of the outdoor environment provides a wide range of rich learning experiences across all areas of learning. The EYFS (2012) also acknowledges three characteristics of effective learning that are of particular importance to very young children since they provide the underpinning foundation for successful lifelong learning. Table 1.1 sets out the ways in which the outdoor environment nurtures the characteristics of effective learning and supports play and learning within the prime and specific areas. It includes extracts from the original EYFS in-depth guidance that remain valid within the revised EYFS.

What is the role of practitioners outdoors?

One of the three vision statements for high quality outdoor play describes the adult as 'knowledgeable and enthusiastic' and 'crucial to unlocking the potential of the outdoors'. Ten years ago one of the key aims of the Space to Grow project was to increase practitioner confidence, motivation and enthusiasm for providing high quality play for their children outdoors. For many early years practitioners today this aim is still a priority, and their role as an effective practitioner remains an ongoing concern.

Small changes can improve the support offered to children outdoors; start by observing what the children are currently doing, since this provides useful insights and direct messages about their interests and enthusiasms. Through further observation it is possible to determine what children know already and what experiences they need next. Then, having observed children involved in outside play, it is straightforward to plan what to do next. Focus on observing and identifying the children's interests, and shape ideas for future sessions through these observations. Outline plans for future sessions should emerge out of the children's current play and activities. Other children may join in the play, and more materials brought in by the practitioner will further develop the activity. Through collaboration with the children, developed from ongoing observations, it will be possible to create a stimulating outdoor environment, a mixture of planned provision, and child-initiated play that supports learning across all areas of the curriculum.

Table 1.1

How does the outdoor environment nurture the characteristics of effective learning and support curriculum delivery?		
Playing and exploring Environments that provide opportunities for playing and exploring foster children's curiosity and satisfy their built-in drive to speculate, test out their theories and seek answers to self-posed questions. It enables children to develop and refine their ideas by combining their existing understandings with new learning. The outdoor environment provides a natural context for children's play and explorations. It is a space where children can get involved in 'actively constructing knowledge and understanding through playful qualities of engaging with their environment and with others' (Tickell 2011). It is an ever-changing space with innate challenges and risks. It supports experimentation and speculation, and can be modified and adapted through the seasons and according to children's interests and enthusiasms.	*Active learning* Outdoor environments that enable active learning support children's attempts to make sense of their surroundings and solve problems, and motivate them to concentrate, persevere and enjoy achieving what they set out to do. Active investigation of their daily experiences is how babies and children begin to make sense of their world. It is through engaging in active learning experiences that they become confident, successful learners who make a responsible and positive contribution to their community. They are able to use their imagination, tackle new experiences and develop new knowledge, understandings and skills. They can confidently follow their own interests, overcome obstacles in order to reach their goals, self-assess and manage risk safely, and enjoy a sense of purpose and achievement. They learn how to respect and work alongside others, how to tackle problems, communicate, negotiate and share decision making.	*Creating and thinking critically* A well-resourced and stimulating outdoor environment offers children direct contact with nature and can be a catalyst for creativity as children can develop their own ideas, choose from a wide range of experiences and make independent decisions about their play. Problems can be explored, discussed and worked through alone, with playmates or with a supporting practitioner. Boundaries are clear and understood by all, allowing risks to be assessed, and adventures embarked upon. Outdoors offers children the conditions for unstructured play and learning through which their skills in creating and thinking critically can flourish.

Table 1.1 continued

How does the outdoor environment support the 'prime areas'?		
Personal, social emotional development	**Communication and language**	**Physical development**
The unique and special nature of the outdoors brings opportunities to experience beauty, joy, wonder and exuberance into children's everyday lives. Outdoors provides a safe supervised place for children to explore new challenges, learn to manage risk and to cope with change and adversity. Outdoor play offers meaningful opportunities for personal independence as children learn to manage outdoor clothing. Social relationships can be developed in a space that offers scope for communication through action, movement and language. Shared enterprises can be undertaken and emerging problems can be discussed and resolved. Negotiating for equipment or turns offers children situations where they can learn to consider the needs of others.	The outdoor environment offers children opportunities to speak and listen in a range of situations and to develop their confidence and skills in expressing themselves. Providing place where talk can happen is crucial. Smaller enclosed spaces such as dens and camps will offer a secluded place for conversations. Collaborative play activities will encourage discussions and problem solving amongst children. One of the most important outdoor experiences practitioners can provide for children is to take the time to talk with and listen to them. Through these relaxed conversations children begin to learn about themselves and their world. Practitioners need to communicate in a way that relates to the age and interests of the child. Understanding what children like to do outdoors and knowing how children of different ages communicate is crucial for rewarding interaction with them.	The outdoors is a place where children can move and handle resources, and develop control and dexterity with tools and small equipment, for example, through digging and gardening, or using bats and balls, hammers and nails, mark-making activities and sand play equipment. In the outdoor environment children can be physically active on a larger scale than is possible indoors. There are exciting opportunities for purposeful movement over large areas, exploration of different levels, negotiation along pathways and around objects, and changes in direction and speed. The outdoors supports children's developing awareness of personal health and self-care, for example through 'sun safe' routines in hot weather, and hygiene routines after handling earth. They can experience the effect of physical activity on their bodies, as their hearts beat faster and they breathe more deeply after vigorous movement. They can experience the reverse effect as they lie quietly on a rug outdoors.

Table 1.1 continued

How does the outdoor environment support the 'specific areas'?			
Literacy	**Mathematics**	**Understanding of the world**	**Expressive arts and design**
The outdoors is a place where stories, songs and poems can be shared and enacted. Mark-making opportunities can be messy and large-scale using mud and water. Babies and toddlers will enjoy making handprints in damp sand, while older children can set a trail of sticks round the outdoor area leading to their den. Natural materials can be used as symbols in children's imaginative play and thus support their emergence of skills needed for reading. The outdoors offers babies, toddlers and young children exciting opportunities for developing upper body and limb strength through physical activity and movement. These experiences will have a positive impact on the development of control and coordination of small muscles needed later for successful handwriting.	The outdoor environment is a place where children can enjoy number rhymes and number games. They can discover the significance of numbers as they count how many beans have grown on the beanstalk and work out whether there are enough for everyone to try one. Natural materials, such as twigs, conkers, chestnuts and pebbles can be sorted and graded according to size or shape. Children develop understanding of mathematical language and concepts in real life situations, for example, deciding how many more umbrellas or Wellington boots are needed if another two children want to go out on a rainy day. Perceptions and theories about shape, space and measure can be tried and tested as babies crawl between bushes, toddlers fill buckets with stones, or older children create patterns with fir cones.	The outdoor environment offers children first-hand experience of nature through touching plants, smelling flowers, crawling on earth and watching the movements of insects, spiders or beetle. The cycle of plant growth and seasonal changes, the impact of wind, weather and seasons can all be experienced directly. The outdoors offers a meaningful context for using simple ICT, for example a walkie talkie to contact a friend hidden in the den, or a camera to photograph a spider's web. Use of the outdoors widens children's sense of people and community as they move between indoors and outdoors, watch passing people or cars, and note the features of their immediate and wider environment. Outdoors can be the setting for affirming events and traditions that contribute to children's growing awareness of their culture and community.	The outdoors is a place where children of all ages can explore and investigate a wide range of materials. Children can satisfy their curiosity in how things work through practical investigations, for example, what happens when a tower of logs falls down, or why balls only roll downhill. They can work out how materials can be joined to achieve a pre-planned purpose, for example, creating a structure on which they can balance. Through language and music, dance and movement, art and role-play props they can express and communicate their ideas and feelings. Outdoors, children can experiment with materials and repeat patterns of play. They can explore different materials in two and three dimensions and apply existing knowledge to new situations and become questioning and inventive thinkers.

Working with babies and toddlers outdoors

Observation of babies and toddlers outdoors reveals how they use their bodies, senses and materials imaginatively and creatively. They have a noticeable fascination with natural materials as well as free and found resources. Supportive adults offer many experiences to develop and extend young children's expanding imagination and creativity. Careful observation of their interests and enthusiasms enables adults to support and encourage toddlers further in their endeavours.

Very young babies respond to people and situations with their whole bodies. They are competent in observing and responding to their immediate environment. Allow babies to lie, roll or crawl on different tactile surfaces, such as grass, rubber, stone, sand or snow, and provide babies with a selection of different materials, such as pebbles, shells or leaves, which allow them to make choices and explore with feet and hands. When playing with babies, sit closely or hold them, carrying them to explore together the objects or materials, talking to them about what they are doing.

As they get a bit older, babies' explorations become more intentional. Increasing mobility and language development enable them to find out and understand more about their world. Provide materials that involve using all the senses, and allow babies and toddlers to play both independently and as a group. Be aware of the ways in which babies communicate what they need, such as pointing and flapping hands, or looking and babbling at the desired item. Provide containers such as bags or buckets to allow them to transport materials from one place to another. Provide opportunities for babies to splash in puddles, tread in leaves or move in snow. Draw their attention to sounds such as splashing water, rustling leaves, wind chimes, birds or animals and traffic noises. Encourage them to listen and note the way they show you they have understood, through their verbal and non-verbal responses.

Once they are more mobile young children begin to show obvious pleasure in moving, communicating and learning through play. Support toddlers to experiment with combining materials such as sand, soil and water. Provide more opportunity for them to transport materials from one area to another. Encourage them to really investigate and talk about these experiences. Note how they use their senses and the creative ways in which they use new language, sometimes combining words to make meaning.

Between two and three years, children's competence at moving, talking and pretending is increasingly evident and they show confidence in themselves and their abilities. Investigate the environment with them and discuss with them what resources they need and

where they might find them. Encourage them to solve problems and make decisions for themselves, such as how to move the leaves from a path, enlarge a puddle or collect dripping water from a tap. Explore under stones and through collections of dead leaves for mini-beasts. Examine plants, twigs and stones and observe insects, butterflies and bees. Listen to what children say, describe and predict what they do, act as their interpreters and respond to their questions. As children learn to do things for themselves they gain confidence knowing you are close by, ready to support and help them if need be.

Working with three- to five-year-olds outdoors

Enabling outdoor environments provide the context for adults and children to work together. In the EYFS (2007) it was recognised that 'outdoor learning is more effective when adults focus on what children need to be able to do there rather than identifying what children need to have'. Furthermore it was argued that 'an approach that considers experiences rather than equipment places children at the centre of the provision for outdoor learning and ensures that individual children's learning and developmental needs are taken account of and met effectively' (Effective practice: Outdoor Learning, EYFS 2007). Child-

ren's outdoor learning is enhanced by the effective support of practitioners in an environment that is richly resourced, with exciting play materials and open-ended flexible resources that can be adapted and used in different ways, according to the needs and interests of individual children.

Learning through Landscapes identified that effective outdoor educators:

- let the children take the lead in planning for outdoor play activities;
- support children by creating and developing an exciting and stimulating outdoor area that builds on their interests;
- take time to discover a completely different side to the child who has remained quiet and introverted indoors;
- welcome the increase in noise levels and conversations as children enjoy the freedom of outdoors;
- join in with the children – play alongside them, ask questions and introduce new ideas, language and skills;
- take a genuine and enthusiastic interest in the children's own world of outdoor play;
- have fun and enjoy being outside;
- value the impact of exercise outdoors on the health and well-being of both the children and the adults.

The booklet, *Learning, Playing and Interacting: Good Practice in the Early Years Foundation Stage* (DCSF 00775-2009 BKT-EN) asserts that skilled and thoughtful practitioners will display many of the following characteristics and skills:

- they will facilitate children's extended use of outdoor spaces, ensuring children have sustained time to develop their own activities, joining in sensitively and following children's play agendas; they will model the thinking processes and skills and work collaboratively with children to promote new knowledge and understandings. They will show genuine interest in the children's ideas, celebrate their interests and achievements, and be proactive in identifying their next steps; they will be sensitive to each child's thinking; allowing them time and valuing their suggestions. Practitioners will scaffold children's outdoor learning through talk, discussing strategies and ideas, suggesting possibilities and modelling approaches. They will support children to persevere through difficulties, to take risks, and to resolve their own conflicts. They will provide children with first-hand experiences to explore

and discover, and they will replenish and vary resources to maintain children's interests and provoke new ideas.

Chapter 6 includes further information about the characteristics and skills needed by the workforce and photocopiable self-reflection tools to help practitioners evaluate their own practice and identify areas for professional development.

2 Getting started

Changing and developing the outdoor environment

Learning through Landscapes advocates that co-operation and involvement lie at the heart of any plan to improve the outdoor environment. For maximum success, outdoor play projects require the combined efforts of everyone: teaching and non-teaching staff, governors/management committee, children and parents.

The process of change and development is based on three underlying principles. Changes must be

- holistic: involving consideration of the whole site, the whole child, the whole setting community (i.e. children, parents, staff, management) and the whole curriculum (i.e. learning experiences that are planned or unplanned, as well as those that are child-initiated or adult-directed);
- participative: experience has shown that the most successful developments have involved children with adults in all aspects of the project, including the development of ideas, decision-making, helping with practical projects, and longer-term maintenance and evaluation of the project;
- sustainable: as well as aiming to use sustainable principles and practices, consideration must be given to the management and maintenance of the outdoor space in the longer term. This will ensure that what has been initially achieved continues to develop and be of benefit to others in the future.

The outdoor area at Ditton Church Preschool at the beginning of the project

These three principles provide the context for making changes to the use of outdoors. However, Learning through Landscapes has also developed a step-by-step process to guide and support early years practitioners wishing to develop their outdoor spaces. The following chapters look at that process in detail and give examples of how it was implemented in Kent.

Telling people about the project

Getting everyone enthusiastic and committed to the project is a very valuable first step. It ensures that the responsibility for the project does not fall solely on a few individuals and enables identification of people with useful skills. The chair of the management committee at Little

Acorns (Herne) Preschool recognised that the commitment of the staff, the committee and the parents was essential to ensure the progress and success of any outdoor developments. So, before formally joining the project, the committee canvassed for parental support at their Annual General Meeting. Having established that parents were in favour of becoming part of the Space to Grow project, the chair and supervisor arranged for a presentation about the project to be shared with staff to inspire them with ideas and to show what could be achieved. Spending time on these preliminary meetings ensured that everyone was aware and committed from the outset.

...and after six months hard work!

In March 2004 Learning through Landscapes conducted a six-month review of the Space to Grow project, to identify what had been learnt and achieved and to provide a focus for the remainder of the project. All those involved in the review meetings were asked to complete a time-line showing their personal highs and lows and the identifying factors attributable to these feelings. Table 2.1 shows a summary of the comments made during the review. One of the key messages to come out of this review highlights the importance of involving others and sharing the workload.

There are many effective ways to canvass support and ensure that everyone is involved in the process. Examples include

- talking with the children at Circle Time;
- giving a presentation to all staff and the management team;
- holding an information evening for parents and the local community;
- sending a publicity flyer home with each child;
- mounting a display;
- involving the local media;
- including an article or an advertisement in the parents' newsletter or on the setting's website.

The Kent settings recognised the need to enthuse parents about the benefits of regular access to outdoor provision. Those settings that successfully shared with parents the benefits of learning through play outdoors found that, as parents became increasingly skilled at recognising the learning that was taking place outdoors, they became more interested in their children's activities in that space.

Table 2.1 Kent Space to Grow project six-month review: summary of positives and negatives

Positive factors and influences	Negative factors and influences
• Being part of something bigger • Inspiration from other places/people • Support from a wider body of people – parents, management, staff • Positive feedback from others – staff, children, parents • Having some initial successes • Getting started • Visual changes • Noticing the impact on children's learning/behaviour/development	• Delays • Unrealistic timescales • Lack of support from parents, staff • Other demands on time • Extra workload • Unreliable contractors • Costs – spiralling/unforeseen/underestimated • Red tape from regulatory bodies • Weather • Concerns about vandalism and security • Unrelated factors, e.g. staff sickness, Ofsted inspections

Identifying who can help

It is useful to conduct a skills audit in the early stages of the project to ascertain who might be able to do what and to encourage as many people as possible to get involved. The list below is not exhaustive but it includes some of the skills that may be needed as the project progresses.

- gardening
- designing
- artwork
- letter writing
- fundraising
- catering
- carpentry
- creche organisation
- bookkeeping
- first aid
- computing skills

Bedgebury Junior School Foundation Stage play area

Try a range of approaches to identify the people with the right skills. Ditton Church Preschool had a very positive response to a letter they sent to parents and friends of the school and members of Ditton Church (see Figure 2.1). However, other settings had more success by making a direct and personal request to individuals. For example, Sunshine and Showers Nursery School had success in persuading the regulars at their local pub to support their project plans. The Foundation Stage staff at Bedgebury Junior School held a very successful coffee morning for parents, to provide information about the project. Key members of the school community were also invited; for example, a member of the team responsible for maintaining the school grounds, and the bursar. This ensured that the whole school community was aware and involved from the outset and helped secure ongoing support for the project.

July 2003

Dear Parents/Friends of Ditton Church Preschool/Members of Ditton Church

I have great pleasure in announcing that we are 1 of 15 schools from 150 applications that have been selected to be part of an Outdoor Play Project led by Learning through Landscapes and Kent Early Years Childcare Unit.

Funding will be available for use to renovate our rear garden to develop a safe, secure and stimulating outdoor play and learning area, where all aspects of the foundation stage curriculum can be provided.

We need the following from everyone:

- Ideas – What would you like to see in the garden?
- Your children's ideas – What would they like to see in their garden?
- Your knowledge and advice – Have we any builders/gardeners/ carpenters that would help with advice, practical help or lend equipment?
- Your muscle – We do need to have an element of voluntary work for the funding to be fully released – can you spare an hour or two over the holidays to help clear the garden?
- Your contacts – Do you know anyone that could be helpful in a project like this?

We would all be very grateful if you could help in any way as we are thrilled to be part of such a great project that will benefit all that use the Church Centre.

Figure 2.1 Letter sent from Ditton Church Preschool

Co-ordinating the project

It is very useful to establish a group of interested people to co-ordinate the project as it progresses. This project team can make and review plans, delegate tasks, organise events, and provide a focus for feedback, discussion and decision-making. It is a good idea to allocate specific roles to team members so that each person has a clear responsibility for action and feedback.

Members of the project team could include:

- senior staff, for example preschool leader, head teacher, officer-in-charge;
- teaching staff;
- non-teaching staff, for example caretaker/grounds person, midday supervisors, administrative staff;
- management, for example a preschool committee member or school governor;
- parents, who will also be able to contribute valuable insights into their child's perspective;
- as appropriate, external organisations, for example a representative from the EYDCP, volunteer groups, or environmental organisations.

Involving everyone in developing the project plans

A base plan showing the external area is very useful when planning improvements. It can be used to map what exists on the site at present. At Bertie's Playgroup in Faversham the staff created a plan of the outdoor area and highlighted the existing features (see Figure 2.2). This plan was then used as the starting point for consultations and planning regarding the future use of the space.

Aim to record everything on the plan: trees, buildings and fences, access routes, cultivated

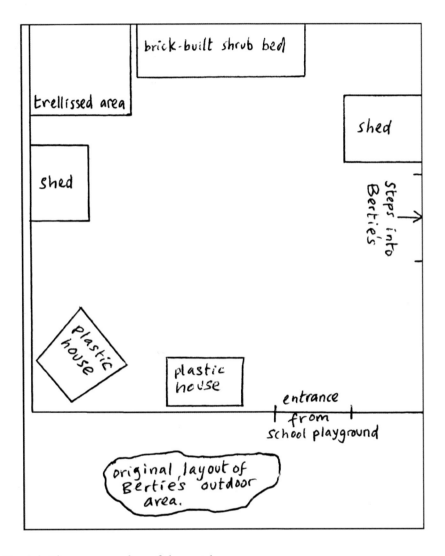

Figure 2.2 Bertie's Playgroup – plan of the outdoor area

areas, seating and any existing fixed play equipment. Include the features that are to be kept and those that may be removed. An enthusiast within the setting can draft scale site plans, or it may be possible to obtain plans from the local authority. If landscaping changes are being made, more detailed information will be required about the location and existence of underground and over-head services, for example water, gas, electricity, telephone, drains. This information is obtainable from the relevant local utility companies.

Once the plan of the existing features has been completed, keep one copy as a master version, and make several copies to use as working documents.

Involving staff

Gathering the views of staff is an important stage in the development of the project. Asking staff to identify the positive and negative aspects of the outdoor area often reveals differences of opinion and raises some interesting points for discussion. For example, Table 2.2 shows that the large outdoor space is seen as positive by some staff who recognise the freedom it offers children. However, it is also seen as a negative feature by staff with concerns about maintaining appropriate levels of supervision. Discussion and resolution of these issues is an integral part of the process of developing the use and management of the outdoor space.

Table 2.2 Examples of typical comments from staff about the outdoor environment

Positive aspects	Negative aspects
• Safe and secure • Variety of surfaces including tarmac and grass • Big fixed equipment • Plants and trees • Large space children can go anywhere • Children love being outdoors	• Bike play lacks purpose • Sheds are not in a good position • Static equipment has less flexibility and play value • Wet grass – gets muddy, have to keep children off it • Supervision difficult – can't see all the children all the time • Have to be outdoors too long – gets cold in the winter

Before making any changes it is important to find out how the outdoor space is used at present to support children's learning. Ask staff to consider how they would like to extend the use of outdoors in the future. Analyse curriculum plans to identify which aspects of learning take place outdoors, when and where, as well as any gaps in the existing provision.

The first step towards curriculum development is a review of the existing possibilities for learning. By taking stock of everything that is already present in the outdoor space, including features such as plants, surfaces, walls and raised areas, staff will have a clearer awareness of the existing potential for supporting children's learning. For example, walls can be used for large-scale painting activities, traverse climbing, chalking and exploration of texture (see Figure 2.3).

This review will also help the project team identify the issues that are currently preventing staff from making the best use of the outdoor space; for example, difficult access, shared use of the space, lack of shade. Record the outcomes of these discussions with staff for future reference as the project progresses. Learning through Landscapes provides a useful audit sheet activity as part of its support for members of Early Years Outdoors. Several settings made good use of the audit activity to review their outdoor space. At Glebe House Day Nursery the owner commented, 'The audit was very useful, it seemed hard at first but once we had completed it, it really helped us formulate our plans.'

If the outdoor space is not currently being used at all, discuss with staff what initial changes would enable them to begin to support Foundation Stage learning outdoors. Their response may focus on practical issues, for example inadequate fencing, or lack of resources. There may be organisational difficulties related to deployment or storage. Alternatively, the poor use of

Case study 2.1 Gathering the views of staff: Victoria Road Primary School

The Reception children at Victoria Road Primary School in Ashford use a mobile classroom sited at the edge of the school playground. The teaching staff were very keen to provide them with access to an outdoor environment for learning, and prior to the project they had already reclaimed a small unused courtyard behind the mobile classroom. This allowed small groups of children to take turns to have access to outdoors. However, it was not big enough to accommodate all children and support outdoor learning across all areas of the Foundation Stage curriculum.

Developing the Reception children's use of the large playground during lesson time was being considered as an option for improving their access to outdoors. However, consultation with staff revealed their concerns about using this space. The key issues identified by staff focused on the following aspects:

- the playground in its current state was a bleak and barren environment;
- the playground did not support a wide range of experiences to nurture children's knowledge and understanding of the world; in particular there were few opportunities for children to experience the natural world.

The provision for children's creative development would be ineffective since the playground lacked features to support this aspect of children's learning. The views of staff were noted and provided a vital insight into the problems that needed addressing through the project.

outdoors may be linked to a lack of confidence among staff in relation to their own role outdoors. At St Martin's Preschool Group, Dover, staff and children were already making some good use of outdoors, however their willingness to initiate further improvements to their outdoor space was hampered by uncertainties about the group's long-term viability (see Chapter 4, Case study 4.13).

Whatever the concerns, the project team will need to support staff to identify the underlying reasons and then make effective use of this information to guide the project focus.

Involving children

Equally important is an evaluation of the children's use of the existing space. If the consultation process is meaningful to them, children will be able to provide valuable input to the project. However, to be truly effective, the skill of listening to and consulting with young children must

This part of the audit is to help you evaluate the PHYSICAL and AESTHETIC qualities of the outdoor space you have access to.

Auditing the physical environment	What happens now? What is the existing provision? Who is using it? What experiences do children currently have? How are adults involved?	How well does this work for us? What is working well? What is less effective?	What limits this? What makes it difficult, limits or prevents us from improving this aspect? i.e. space / staffing / cash / resources / H&S / other?	How could this be made better? What could we do to develop children's use of our outdoor space? i.e. space planning / staff development/ developing resources / other?
How easy is it for our children to move between indoors and outdoors?	Mostly free-flow. 3 steps + adult support.	Summer - easier. doors + steps in winter.	transition area awkward to access. H&S - steps and door.	ease of accessing coats – poss. relocate.
How easy is it to set up/clear away equipment and activities outside?	2 sheds—adult access all activities ∴ adult initiated	variety of equip. difficult to set-up.	space + access to sheds.	child access to resources. more variety. Don't require equip
Do we have adequate, safe, secure outdoor storage areas?	2 sheds – safe and secure.	safe + secure	could be bigger with better access.	get more adequate storage.
Do we have a variety of surfaces, textures, colours and shapes?	tarmac. Coloured plastic equip	Can use all year. Is not used effic. all year. Lack of variety.	ideas, resources	provide more of...
Do we have a secure and attractive site boundary?	secure fence boundary.	more could be made of the boundary as a resource.	Cash & resources.	Could be made more attractive.
Do we provide a special area for babies and toddlers?	N/A		N/A	
Do we have interesting views out of our site?	into school & ground. Some green & trees.	children can see through fence—see their siblings.		
Have we any seating areas?	the plastic picnic bench.	Is portable but is plastic + limited.	space, ideas!	ask children where they would like to sit.
Do we make the most of our planted/green spaces?	Planted border pots all adult initiated no trees/child tended.	have space for planting/child gardening opportunities.	knowledge + ideas.	input from green-fingered person!
Do we have any shade or shelter?	No shade/shelter	childn can't play out if too hot/rainy.	cash + resources, ideas.	shelter from rain shade from sun.
How are we catering for children's physical play needs?	all ch'n have access + use of resources + adults support.	childn make use of resources. equip. Not enough climbing/jumping etc.	resources	plan for all aspects of physic-al play.

Figure 2.3 Auditing the physical environment – Bertie's Playgroup

be embedded in everyday practice. If adults go through the motions of listening yet do not enable children to make a difference to the direction of the project, the consultation process will be meaningless and frustrating. Children will quickly be discouraged from expressing their views if they feel that their participation has neither been taken into account nor respected. At the end of each chapter the strategies and ideas used within the Space to Grow project for gathering the views and perspectives of children are set out in a series of prompt sheets. The final section of the book includes recommendations for essential further reading for further information and a greater understanding of useful techniques.

Children outdoors at Happy Faces Preschool

As part of the Space to Grow project, the settings were encouraged to involve children in the development of the outdoor space. Settings were asked to find out how children felt about their existing outdoor space, and identify how they used it at the time. The Reception children at Victoria Road Primary School were asked what they liked and disliked about their existing outdoor space (see Figure 2.4).

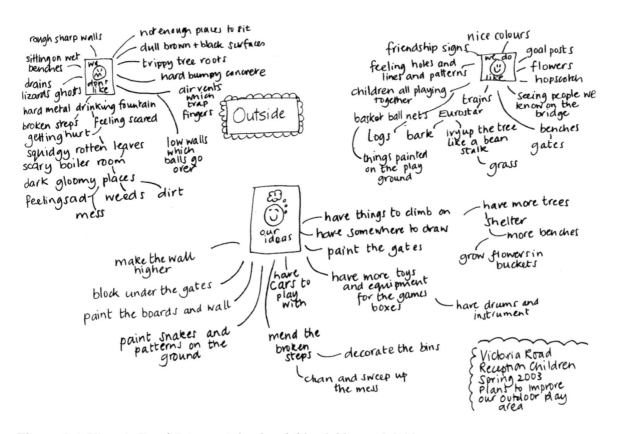

Figure 2.4 Victoria Road Primary School – children's likes and dislikes

Settings were asked to observe children and collect information on the types of activities the children engaged in while outdoors – both adult-planned and child-initiated.

They noted how children used the space, where they went and how all these play activities impacted on each other. They considered whether children had a wide range of outdoor opportunities and experiences over time. They reflected on whether any of these experiences were particularly important for the children attending, and therefore a priority for further development.

In several settings, children were given disposable cameras to take photographs of the outdoor places that were important to them. Once developed, these pictures were used to stimulate further discussion. Each child talked about their photographs, made comments and answered questions about their views on future changes to the space (see Case study 2.2).

Case study 2.2 Gathering children's perspectives: Happy Faces Preschool

The Kent Space to Grow project incorporated a pilot research project, Spaces to Play. The Thomas Coram Research Unit carried out this pilot study at Happy Faces Preschool. The children worked with the researcher to explore their understanding and use of outdoor provision, in order to inform the process of change to their outdoor play space. The pilot used the Mosaic approach, which combines the traditional research tools of observation and interviewing with participatory methods, including the use of cameras (Clark and Moss 2001). Children were given single-use or cheap reusable cameras and were asked to 'take photographs of what is important here'. The children's choice of subject for their pictures was wide ranging and reflected their different priorities. For example, some children focused on taking pictures of their friends in different parts of the garden, whereas other children concentrated on capturing images of their favourite pieces of equipment. Many children included images of the sky and the perimeter fencing, this recurring theme emphasised to adults how children's outdoor experiences were being dominated by the imposing fencing.

The developed photographs were discussed at length and these conversations provided further insights. Individual children chose particular photographs of their outdoor space to make into a book and these books were shared with others in the setting. The work with cameras provided invaluable information about children's perspectives of their space and enabled the researcher and staff to reflect on the direction for future developments in the preschool.

Alison Clark discussing photographs at Happy Faces Preschool

At Sticky Fingers Day Nursery staff came to realise the importance of asking children what they wanted to **do** outdoors rather what they would like to **have.** The children's wish-list in response to the second question included 'a slide up to the clouds' – a lovely idea but not easily provided in any setting! (see Case study 2.3)

Case study 2.3 **Gathering ideas from children: Sticky Fingers Day Nursery**

The staff at Sticky Fingers Day Nursery were keen to gather ideas from children as part of their initial consultations about the development of the garden. The children were asked two questions and their answers illustrate the importance of asking the right question in the first place.

When asked what they would like to have in their garden their responses included the following ideas:

'a big big trampoline'
'a really big climbing frame with lots of things on it'
'a slide up to the clouds'
'swings and a see-saw'
'a house or a bus or a train or anything with things you can sit on and pictures on the wall'.

Children were also asked what they would like to be able to do outside. Their responses included the following comments:

'run around'
'chalk on the floor'
'just play in it'
'have fun'
'play hide and seek with tents'
'do digging and planting'.

The staff realised that children's responses to this question provided a much more useful starting point for future developments in the garden and included these ideas in their initial planning for the outdoor environment.

In some settings, where children were not currently going into the space earmarked for development, the staff had a harder challenge. How were they to consult children in a meaningful way about outdoors if it was not currently accessible? In Ditton Church Preschool (see Case study 2.4), where the garden was not currently used at all, staff and parents took children to an alternative outdoor environment to observe their interests. The visit provided staff with a wealth of information about children's enthusiasms, which was then incorporated into their own project plans.

Case study 2.4 Involving children: Ditton Church Preschool

Ditton Church Preschool is situated in the Church Centre in Ditton village. It has been open for nearly four years and originally the only outdoor space available to staff and children was the car park at the front of the Church Centre. This enabled some outdoor play, for example with tricycles and balls, but it was not a suitable space for supporting the full range of learning experiences outdoors. However, in July 2003 the preschool were given permission to use part of the garden at the rear of the building. A tour of the space revealed an enormous task ahead – the garden was totally overgrown with nettles and brambles. Rubbish would have to be removed, fences installed and storage repositioned before the staff could begin to think about using the garden to enrich children's learning within the Foundation Stage curriculum.

At the beginning of the project one of the most important stages was to identify the children's priorities for the garden – not an easy task when they weren't able to go out into the space! A decision was made to take the children to visit an organic garden nearby at Yalding and observe them in action. This visit was a resounding success and gave the project team very clear messages about children's perspectives. Children liked to run, balance and jump; they liked to be with their friends; they liked to have hideaways; they were interested in making sounds, sharing new experiences, digging in earth and planting. The children's interests were then incorporated into the plans for the garden and the project team realised that the way forward did not have to involve costly pieces of equipment. Their observations of children outdoors had helped them to recognise that the children's play and learning experiences could be provided for through low-cost resources that were modifiable according to their current interests.

Early years staff working with babies and children under two years old had a similar challenge. How were they to gather the perspectives of these very young children, many of whom had only limited verbal skills and not all of whom were mobile? In Glebe House Day Nursery staff working in the baby room built up a detailed picture of each child's perspective using a range of approaches (see Case study 2.5). Mary Sheridan Preschool provides for children with special educational needs. The staff there used very similar techniques to give the children in their setting a 'voice' in the consultation process (see list of further reading for more information on working with babies and children with special educational needs).

Case study 2.5 **Gathering views of babies and children under two years old: Glebe House Day Nursery**

The babies and toddlers at Glebe House Day Nursery share use of the large garden with older children. They also have direct access from the Baby Room to a secluded balcony area for outdoor play. However, the space is undeveloped and underused so staff were keen to rectify this situation as part of their outdoor developments.

Below is a summary of the range of approaches used by staff to give even the very youngest children a 'voice' in the consultation process.

'Tuning in' to very young children

Key staff working directly with babies and toddlers were already naturally 'tuning in' to their interests and needs and through this daily interaction they identified several significant issues. The children were particularly interested in posting and retrieving objects from containers and boxes. They also liked pulling themselves up to standing position and 'cruising' round fixed objects.

Talking to parents

The Nursery staff in the Baby Room had a good rapport with parents, so it was easy to find out about children's outdoor activities and experiences elsewhere, for example in the local park or in the garden at home. Parents commented that children liked equipment that included opportunities to experience motion, such as rocking, rolling and see-sawing.

Observations

The Nursery implements an observation and assessment system that tracks children's progress towards developmental milestones. This record is used to help key workers plan further experiences that support the learning needs of individual children in their care. So each key worker contributed useful information to the consultation process.

The babies and toddlers at Glebe House Day Nursery were given a 'voice' by staff through a process that gathered information about their interests, preferences and concerns from as many sources as possible. Staff took time to really 'listen' and interpret these messages before focusing on developing their plans for outdoors. Inspiration from *Early Years Outdoors* and early years magazines provided staff with a useful focus for further discussion at team meetings and assisted them in implementing the next stage of their outdoor project.

   Children can also participate in surveys of the outdoor area. Encourage them to identify hazards, find the shady or sunny areas, or record where water collects after rain. Consider providing disposable cameras for a photographic survey resulting in a display showing children's most and least favourite areas of the outdoor space. St John's Primary School and Preschool used specific props to provide a focus for children's thoughts during the survey and make the activity more meaningful (see Case study 2.6).

Case study 2.6 Involving children in surveying the space: St John's Preschool and Primary School

Children in the preschool and in the Reception class have adjoining classrooms and share use of the outdoor area. As part of the initial stages of their project, the staff were keen to involve children in surveying the space. A session was planned that involved children from both the preschool and the Reception class. The purpose of the activity was to explore with children how they viewed the existing space and to identify how it could be improved upon.

Using information gathered from earlier conversations with children about outdoors, staff decided to concentrate the session on identifying *places to dig*, *places to paint*, *places to hide*, and *places to run*. Simple props were made available to provide a focus for children's thinking, i.e. trowels, paintbrushes, cuddly toys and trainers. Children worked in small groups with an adult to discuss and identify the best options for these experiences. The information was then recorded using symbols on a plan of the outdoor space.

The staff found that the session revealed some interesting information, for example, all the children except one showed a clear preference for painting on vertical spaces, such as walls, windows and doors. Staff had to then evaluate whether this preference had arisen because of the existing lack of horizontal places for painting, or because children valued the extra opportunities that the outdoor environment provided for using vertical spaces. Taking the time to reflect on the observations made and the information gathered is vital to ensure that the project moves forward in the right direction.

A basket of props to provide a focus for children's thinking

The 'Getting started' prompt sheets at the end of this chapter provide further information and ideas for involving children in the early stages of developing outdoors.

Involving others

It is essential to seek out the opinions of other people. Include those people directly involved in the setting, such as parents, management and grounds maintenance staff. Also, consider the views of other users of the outdoor environment, for example parent and toddler groups, after-school clubs or youth clubs. The project team at MCNA Preschool realised it is important not to overlook issues that may be of particular significance to other users. Conflict between user groups will arise if future changes have not taken account of everyone's needs (See Case studies 2.7 and 2.8).

Case study 2.7 **Involving others in the development of the outdoor space: MCNA Preschool**

MCNA Preschool is a community group that shares its accommodation and outdoor environment with other user groups in the neighbourhood. Consequently, it was vital that everyone was consulted about the plans for developing the outdoors, to ensure that any potential conflict could be resolved during the project design stage. Once the plans for the garden had been developed, staff shared their ideas with representatives from other user groups within the building.

This revealed a significant problem with the planned layout; the proposed position of the sandpit was going to impact on the space used by children at the after-school club for their football games. However, the ensuing discussions between the preschool and the after-school club led to a mutually agreeable compromise option and the design plans were adjusted to reflect the new position.

Case study 2.8 **Gathering the views and perspectives of all users of the space: Bedgebury Junior School**

The space used by the nursery children was also used by older children, during break-time and lunchtime. Therefore it was vital that any development plans also took account of older children's existing use and their ideas and perspectives. As part of the consultation process children in Years 1 and 2 were asked to share their views through photographs, drawings and conversations. This information was then fed back to the early years staff involved in planning the developments outdoors.

For some settings the initial involvement and agreement of others is an absolute priority. St Martin's Preschool in Folkestone uses a community centre adjacent to a playing field and car park. They needed the landowners to give permission for them to use and develop an area of the site before they could proceed with their plans (see Case study 2.9).

The staff at Saplings @ The Sports Centre had ongoing difficulties in securing their perimeter fencing before further developments could take place. Pupils at the adjacent secondary school kept damaging it in their efforts to retrieve their footballs. Providing a designated access gate for them solved the problem overnight!

Case study 2.9 **Getting permission to use and develop an outdoor space: St Martin's Preschool**

Children at St Martin's Preschool were already making some good use of the car park and adjoining field. However, staff were keen to fence and develop a plot of land outside the community centre for the preschool's sole use, in order to enrich the outdoor curriculum and reduce the amount of time spent on monitoring children's movements and safety on the large playing field.

Initial enquiries revealed that the land was owned by the MOD, managed by the community centre committee, and used by several groups including the local primary school. The supervisor at the preschool recognised that to have any chance of achieving their aim they would have to put a very good case to several organisations.

The preschool spent time carefully preparing their case; they used cones to map out the area under discussion and took photographs for their presentation. They put forward a clear proposal setting out why they needed the space, what they would use it for, how it would be maintained and how the impact on other user groups would be kept to a minimum. At the end of the project in 2005, negotiations were underway and staff were hopeful that an agreement would be reached. Having been in recent contact with the preschool supervisor I am delighted to report that they were successful and now have their own enclosed outdoor space at the edge of the playing field.

St Martin's Preschool is keen to fence a plot of land

Involving children in 'Getting started'

Surveying the existing space: Tours (see Clark and Moss 2005: 37–9)

When to use this activity

Useful technique for:

- active children who like to be on the move;
- identifying favourite spaces in existing environments;
- surveying existing features in the environment;
- identifying features, items or activities of importance to the child.

Use this activity to build up detailed information about what children currently like to do outdoors.

Preparation and resources

Offer children a variety of methods for recording their views during the tour. Options could include:

- cameras;
- clipboards, pencils and paper;
- audio or video tape recorders;
- Dictaphone.

Gathering the information

Individual children take an adult on a tour of the outdoor space. They can be given control of the route of the tour and how their preferences are recorded during the tour, and how they will be documented later.

Ask open questions, such as 'What happens in this part of the garden?'

Making sense of the information

Invite children to share their thoughts with other children or staff. Looking at the photographs, drawings or recordings will promote further discussion about the space and ensure that staff draw an accurate conclusion about children's views.

Issues to consider

Keep an open mind and try not to make assumptions about the information children provide. For example, for some children the importance of particular areas of the garden is strongly linked to whether or not it is associated with social interaction with friends rather than to the equipment that is sited there.

Involving children in 'Getting started'

Using prop sacks and treasure baskets

When to use this activity

Useful technique for:

- identifying children's current perspectives and use of their environment;
- helping very young children to focus on the process and purpose of the consultation
- involving active children who like to be on the move.

Preparation

Gather together a set of resources that will act as a focus for the consultation. Present these items to children in a drawstring sack or a basket. Use equipment that children will easily relate to, objects that they will understand the purpose of, and items for which children will be able to identify a use and context, such as:

picture book	seeds	sunglasses
trowel	watering can	windmill
doll	ball	Wellington boots
car	blanket	paintbrush

Each item is used to gather children's perspectives on a different aspect/feature of the outdoor space.

Gathering the information

An individual child, or a pair of children, works outdoors with an adult. They choose an item from the sack or basket and then find the best place in the garden for the associated experience. For example, a child choosing the book from the basket would show the adult the best place for reading a story outdoors. Similarly, the child choosing sunglasses, a windmill or Wellington boots would find the sunniest, windiest or muddiest spot outdoors.

Making sense of the information

It is important to record the information children provide to allow it to form part of the emerging picture of the way the garden is currently used. A plan of the space is useful. Adults can note where children engage in different types of activities and their views on environmental features, such as sun and wind. Children can also be involved in recording information. Display photographs of the outdoor space and encourage children to stick a symbol or drawing next to the photo that shows the relevant part of the garden.

Issues to consider

Be aware that this may show up unexpected gaps in the existing outdoor provision; for example, if children feel that there is no suitable spot for story-telling. Ensure that any perceived gaps are addressed in the planned developments.

This activity can also be used in the thinking and planning stage with small world toys to identify where proposed new features could be sited (see Prompt sheet 3.1, 'Thinking and planning').

Involving children in 'Getting started'

Surveying the space: tours with an intermediary, such as a puppet or soft toy

When to use this activity

Useful technique for:

- surveying existing features;
- gathering children's perspectives on the existing provision;
- identifying future priorities;
- identifying favourite and important places;
- children under three years old;
- children with limited or undeveloped communication skills.

Use this activity to build up detailed information about what children currently like to do outdoors. The use of an intermediary, such as a named puppet or soft toy, can provide a focus for the survey with very young children. It is also a useful technique if the adult conducting the survey is not well known to the children; they may be reluctant to share their thoughts with an unfamiliar adult but will be happy to talk to the toy. Alternatively, very young children with a limited vocabulary or those with communication difficulties can use the soft toy to show an adult what happens in different parts of the garden (see Clark and Moss 2005: 102).

Preparation and resources

Introduce the puppet or toy, or use one that is already known to the children. It is easier if the puppet has a name for children and adults to refer to it by, for example 'Bertie'.

Consider taking photographs as a record of the survey findings and a catalyst for further discussions among staff and children.

Offer children some options for recording the survey findings, for example through drawings, photographs or tape recordings.

Gathering the information

Individual children take 'Bertie' and an adult on a tour of the outdoor space. Either allow children to choose the route of the tour or ask them to show 'Bertie' where particular experiences take place.

Ask open questions, such as 'Can you show/tell Bertie what happens in this part of the garden?' or 'If Bertie wanted to hide in the garden where would he go?'

Making sense of the information

Invite the children involved in the tour to share their thoughts with other children or staff. Create a book using photographs or children's drawings to promote further discussion about the space. Create a display using 'Bertie' and captioned photographs that identify what children think he could do in each part of the garden.

Issues to consider

Keep an open mind; children's perspectives on the best place for 'Bertie' to go for particular experiences may differ from the adult view. Also, the use of an intermediary can enable children to open up about more sensitive issues, such as why they have strong preferences for, or an aversion to, particular parts of the garden. These insights will need careful consideration by adults involved in planning the future development of the space.

Involving children in 'Getting started'

Interviews

When to use this activity

Useful technique for:

● focusing in on children's perceptions of their everyday experiences;
● gathering responses about a pre-prepared set of questions;
● children who are able to verbalise their thoughts.

Preparation and resources

Work out in advance the questions that will be asked of children. Remember to phrase questions to encourage children to give a full response rather than just 'yes' or 'no'. You may wish to include or adapt the following example questions.

● What is the best thing about outdoors?
● Can you think of anything about outdoors that you don't like?
● Can you think of anything you would like to do outdoors that would make it a better place than it is now?
● Is there anything you want to do outdoors that you are not allowed to do?

Provide a tape recorder to record children's responses.
   (See Clark and Moss 2005: 45–51 for a detailed account of this technique in action.)

Gathering the information

Children participate in a short 'interview' or prepared questions and an adult records their responses. Children should be able to choose the place where the interview takes place. Some may prefer to participate outdoors while others might prefer a familiar spot indoors.

Making sense of the information

Listen to the children's taped responses and note any emerging patterns in their answers. Are there places or features outdoors that are particularly popular or unpopular? What experiences or features have children identified as possible improvements to their outdoor space? Have the interviews highlighted any other matters of importance or concern to children that need to be considered as part of the development plans for outdoors?

Issues to consider

Children may be comfortable being interviewed alone or they may prefer to participate with a friend. Some children will revel in the attention, however not all children will be comfortable with a lengthy session. It is therefore important that children are able to end the interview if they choose to.

Involving children in 'Getting started'

Finding out how children feel about the outdoor environment: happy tokens

When to use this activity

Useful technique for:

- active children who like to be on the move;
- identifying children's preferences in existing environments;
- surveying opinions about existing features in the environment;
- identifying features, items or activities of importance to the child.

Preparation and resources

Gather together several containers and some tokens. The tokens can be anything that is in plentiful supply, for example bricks, beads or buttons. However, take care that the size of the token does not represent a choking hazard to very young children.

Label the containers with a happy or sad face and a note of where they are to be sited. Place them in pairs around the outdoor area in key spots, for example by existing features, such as the climbing frame or the sandpit.

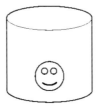

Gathering the information

Encourage children who visit each area to collect a token and drop it into the pot with the face that represents how they feel about the feature or space.

Making sense of the information

By counting the number of tokens in each pot it will be easy to establish preferences for particular areas of the garden. Children can help to count and collate the information onto a summary sheet.

Issues to consider

Some children may not have a strong preference for a particular area. Therefore it may be appropriate to introduce a third pot labelled with a neutral expression to allow these children to express their viewpoint.

It is possible to determine preferences linked to gender or age by giving children preordained tokens; for example, by using a particular colour or shape of token for boys/girls, or for children under/over three years old. This will provide further useful details that can be used to inform future plans.

Involving children in 'Getting started'

Finding out how children feel about the outdoor environment: cheer rating

When to use this activity

Useful technique for:

- active children who like to be on the move;
- identifying children's preferences in existing environments;
- surveying opinions about existing features in the environment;
- identifying features, items or activities of importance to the child.

Preparation and resources

This activity needs little preparation or resources. It is a very useful preliminary activity that can be used to get children used to the process of giving an opinion on aspects of their outdoor environment. Children express their preferences and levels of enthusiasm for different parts of the garden by cheering in each area. A tape recorder is a useful way to record children's responses.

Gathering the information

Having explained the activity to the children, visit each part of the garden with a small group and encourage them to cheer – loudly or quietly according to how they feel about the space. Consider using a tape recorder to document children's responses. Remember to mention on tape where each cheer takes place to help make sense of the recording afterwards.

Making sense of the information

It will be possible to form a general view about how children feel, through their cheer responses. This may confirm the view of adults in the setting or may offer new perspectives.

Issues to consider

This activity does not reveal accurate measurable information; however, it is fun and it will provide a broad overview about how children feel.

3 Thinking and planning

Developing the ideas

This stage of the process focuses on finding ways to develop the use of outdoors as a stimulating learning environment that is fully integrated with the use of indoors. Across the UK, curriculum guidance includes examples of experiences that very young children should have, both indoors and outdoors, and a wealth of ideas for taking learning outdoors. All seven areas of learning can be effectively promoted, and the outdoors is a perfect place for nurturing the characteristics of effective learning. Information about children's current play and learning, gathered through surveys and discussions, provides a good starting point for identifying gaps in the existing outdoor curriculum. These gaps may relate to one aspect of children's development, for example sound-making opportunities, or to a whole area of learning (see Case study 3.1).

However, curriculum development may not be the only focus of the project. Through the earlier stages of the consultation process the project team may have identified other problems that are hampering the development of the outdoor area; for example, limited or undeveloped space, lack of shade, concerns about vandalism or problems with storing equipment. The resolution of these wider issues is an equally important focus for the team and will be crucial to the success of the project. Both Happy Faces Preschool and Sunshine and Showers Nursery School had to make significant changes to their grounds in order to improve children's curriculum experiences outdoors.

Sunshine and Showers Nursery School: a storage area has been transformed

. . . into an outdoor art area!

Case study 3.1 **Enriching the curriculum: Bell Wood Community Primary School**

Bell Wood Community Primary School is at the centre of a dilapidated estate of flats and houses in Maidstone. Many of the children attending the school have few outdoor experiences and little contact with the natural world. In the early years staff had voiced a growing concern about children's under-achievement within the curriculum area promoting understanding of the world. Children's aversion to insects and nature and their lack of respect for living plants and creatures were hampering their learning and progress. This concern was borne out by children's assessments at the end of Reception; analysis showed that children entered the school with very low levels of attainment in this area and, despite the best efforts of staff, at the end of their year in Reception children had not achieved the early learning goals.

A survey among staff, parents and children identified a plot of land in the school that was an underused eyesore and a decision was made to develop this area into a haven for wildlife. Staff recognised that development of the garden is a long-term project and they are aware that it will be some time before they know whether the initiative has achieved their key aim – to improve children's attitudes and experiences of the natural world and improve their attainment. Children have contributed their ideas to a display about the garden and they have helped to select plants at the local garden centre. They have grown seeds, planted them out and watered them during the hot weather. The staff have reviewed the curriculum plans and embedded use of the new wildlife garden into the plans for children's learning to ensure that activities take place throughout the year. Children will be able to use the garden for observational and investigative work. Staff also intend that children will carry out many of the seasonal tasks necessary to tend and maintain the garden throughout the year.

Starting to create a vision plan

A vision plan is a broad outline of the way the outdoor space is to be organised and improved, rather than a detailed plan of the precise developments. It defines the overall layout and structure and supports progress towards making the planned alterations, whether these are changes to the use, management or design of the outdoor area.

Before creating a vision plan it is useful to summarise the issues, problems or areas of conflict that have been identified and need to be resolved. Turn these issues into positive action statements and begin to prioritise them.

It is noticeable in Table 3.1 that some actions relate to management issues, for example staff development, and others involve physical changes, such as improving children's access to shade. Table 3.2 shows how MCNA Preschool turned negative statements into positive action statements that identified what needed to happen next.

Table 3.1 Turning negative issues into positive action

Negative issues	Positive action
● 'The outdoor area is bleak and exposed'	● Create shelter and enclosures
● 'There is not enough shade'	● Improve shade facilities
● 'There are few opportunities for children to grow and care for plants'	● Develop an area for gardening
● 'Equipment keeps being stolen from the shed	● Improve the storage facilities
● 'The staff are not sure of their role outdoors'	● Address staff development needs
● 'Parents complain if the children get muddy'	● Address parental concerns about mud

Table 3.2 MCNA Preschool: turning negative issues into positive action

Negative issue	Positive action	Next step
Lack of safety surface	Install safety surface	● Get two or three quotes for safety surface
No provision for children to explore sounds	Create sound area	● Identify place for sound-making ● Get hold of unwanted saucepans etc.
No provision for children to draw outdoors	Develop mark-making opportunities, fixed and moveable	● Provide blackboards attached to shed ● Supply clipboards and pencils
Insufficient surfaces/ pathways for bikes and wheeled toys	Review and improve provision of bikes and wheeled toys	● Identify minimum width needed to enable children to ride bikes and pass each other ● Work out a scale plan for the cycle track and position of pebble roundabout ● Visit local example of pebbles with children
No provision for children to care for plants/observe seasonal changes in their environment	Develop planted area that changes with the seasons NB After-school club: consider implications for playing football	● Create raised flower bed in corner of garden – therefore minimal impact on football activities and plants given greater protection
No provision for sand play	Provide a sandpit NB consider sunken pit to ensure access by SEN child NB After-school club: consider implications for playing football	● Identify best size and position for new sandpit ● Research manufacturers

Having identified and prioritised the list of positive actions it is useful to circulate this information for comments before moving on to the next stage. Consider displaying the information for parents, sharing it at a staff meeting or management meeting, or publishing it in the next newsletter.

The next step towards the vision plan is the creation of a zone plan (see Figure 3.1). Zoning breaks up larger spaces into more manageable ones, and creates places where activities can be carried out harmoniously. When working out zones, it is better to concentrate on what children would like to be able to **do** in different areas rather than focusing on pieces of equipment to **have** in the space. This enables each solution to have a variety of responses. For example, rather than saying 'we want a sandpit here', settings were encouraged to consider how and where they could offer a variety of digging experiences. See pages 20–1 for experiences that children should be able to DO outdoors. This is a useful starting point for further discussion among staff.

It's important to consider how children move around the play space and provide areas that separate different kinds of experiences, as well as places for children to safely stop and consider what they wish to do next.

The purpose of the zone plan is to:

- identify and define the main areas in the outdoor space;
- site activities and equipment in the best possible location (or zone);
- resolve any major physical site problems and conflicts.

In order to minimise the potential for conflict within the space, ensure that the layout of the area locates complementary zones adjacent to one another. Some settings have zoned their play areas into 'Active – Transition – Quiet'; others have used a 'Work – Rest –Play' division. Each setting's situation is different, so it is essential to involve everyone in this part of the project. See 'Thinking and planning' prompt sheets at the end of this chapter for specific ideas for involving children in this stage of the project. It may take several draft versions to reach the final zone plan that everyone is happy with.

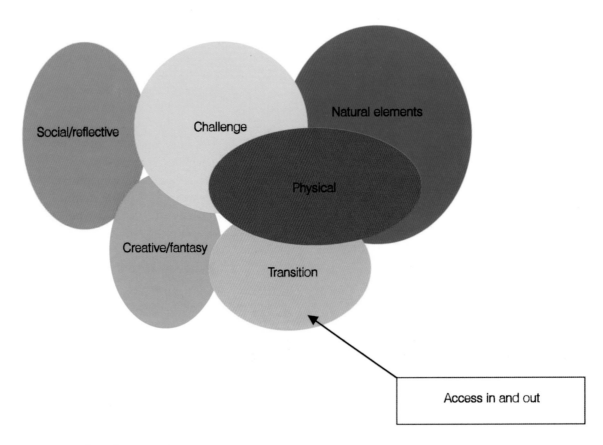

Figure 3.1 Sample zone plan

Source: LTL Developmental Site Visit Service

Useful questions to ask.

- What is the best possible location for a specific use?
- Where else could it be sited?
- What can we shift or change to reduce conflict or improve use?
- Is the space large enough for its purpose?
- Does its location conflict with any of the surrounding uses?
- Does the space have two major uses which will affect its siting?
- Does it need to be near the buildings?
- How will its location affect its maintenance and management?
- Does the orientation of the area affect it?

Once the different zones have been identified and mapped out on the plan, the next step is to find ways of identifying the zones in the actual space, so that staff and children can use each area appropriately and to its full potential. There are many ways of dividing up space, and they don't all involve physical barriers. In many early years settings, space is at a premium, therefore its organisation has to be flexible, to allow for any number of alternative uses. Consequently, it is important to consider ways of defining zones that will enhance the overall effectiveness of the space. For example:

- mark out lines and patterns on the ground – especially good for containing the movement of children on wheelie toys;
- use low hedging or fencing to separate a quiet area;
- temporary zoning can be done using traffic cones, chalk markings or tables, or even milk and bread crates. Children can have fun deciding on a daily or weekly basis where each play zone will be, and turning zone dividers into dens and other play structures;
- a more permanent solution could be to build raised planting beds to divide areas. These also have the advantage of potentially providing greenery in the play area, and allowing children to grow their own plants, or to dig holes and generally get mucky;
- knee rails (a low timber rail which children can also sit on) and bollards can both play a part in zoning spaces.

The project team will need to check the zone plan against the initial site survey information. Make sure that the zone plan takes account of pathways and access routes for vehicles and other users. Ensure that conflicts have been resolved and that where possible special places or important features have been retained or re-sited. Before taking the next step it is useful to make a final copy of the zoning plan and display it prominently for feedback and comments. At Victoria Road Primary School a three-dimensional model of the ideas for the playground was displayed in the school library to allow a wider audience to comment on the plans so far, while at Ditton Church Preschool a more detailed plan was displayed and comments invited from parents (see Figure 3.2).

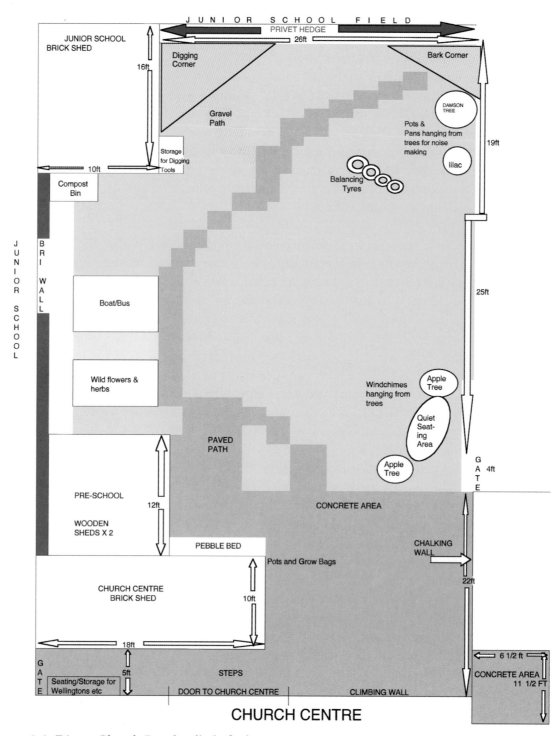

Figure 3.2 Ditton Church Preschool's draft plan

Identifying potential solutions

This stage of the process identifies in detail the potential changes to the use, design or management of the space that are needed. This phase will need to be repeated for each issue in the different areas of the site and the changes may not just be through developing the space and its physical features. In Kent, settings also considered the resources they provided, their planning techniques, the amount and frequency of time that outdoors is available to children and the role and deployment of adults.

As part of the process of finding solutions for each issue it is necessary to identify:

- who needs to be consulted;
- what action needs to be taken;
- who will co-ordinate the action;
- who needs to be contacted about implementation.

The settings had different needs, and the solutions to the problems they faced were wide-ranging and varied. However, it is possible to group some issues into broad categories, such as the following.

Management and organisational changes

These might include changes to the deployment and responsibilities of staff, improving children's access and reorganisation of storage facilities.

Training/increasing knowledge

This may include courses for teaching or non-teaching staff as well as in-service training sessions that look at specific aspects of outdoor provision, for example mathematical development. It may incorporate visits to other settings or outdoor centres for inspiration and exchange of ideas. It may mean collecting and sharing information or materials that support teaching and learning outdoors.

Resources – acquisition or renovation

An audit of existing resources and site features may reveal some that are worn or neglected, as well as highlighting the gaps in current provision. It is important to identify any underlying problems. Why do resources need renewing or replacing? Is storage or vandalism a problem? If so, these issues need addressing before precious funds are spent replacing equipment.

Design solutions – making physical changes

This may include improving seating or shade facilities. It may include the removal of unwanted features, the development of a wildlife garden or the installation of an all-weather canopy.

Gathering everyone's viewpoints on the different options will be vital. Children can offer some very important perspectives on design solutions (see Case study 3.2). For ideas for involving children in identifying design solutions, see 'Thinking and planning' Prompt sheet 3.5.

All weather canopy at Sunshine and Showers Nursery School

Case study 3.2 Involving children in developing designs: Victoria Road Primary School

Having carried out extensive consultations within the whole-school community, the issues were very clear. The children's main concerns focused on the following areas:

- seating;
- ball recovery from the other side of fences and walls;
- den-building facilities;
- stepping stones.

The staff had identified their concerns about:

- the barren environment;
- the children's lack of opportunities to experience the natural world;
- lack of opportunities for creative development.

The wider school community had been consulted and their perspectives were also taken into account and revealed the following information. The playground was also used:

- by older children, therefore any new structures had to be suitable for all ages or removable at break time;
- by midday supervisors pushing trolleys between the kitchen and dining hall;
- as an access route for occasional yet essential oil deliveries.

The next stage was to involve children in developing some solutions that would enrich the playground environment for the Foundation Stage pupils without compromising the requirements of other users of the space. The inspiration for the design session was loosely based around the 'Planning for Real' initiative. This concept has been used successfully to consult with urban communities about the regeneration of their neighbourhood. However, it was necessary to adapt the idea to suit younger participants, so small world toys were used initially to explore some of the design problems. Then, rather than using a small-scale model, staff and children went outside to develop and design solutions within the actual space.

Initially a 'Circle Time' session was used to introduce the idea of a 'Planning for Real' activity. Small-world dolls, construction toys and recyclable materials were used to represent and develop an imaginary playground. This small-world activity focused on the ideas already identified as of concern to the children. Later the same day everyone went outside to explore and experiment with the space in the playground. Each group of six children had an adult supporting them. Each group was asked to develop one area of the playground and find a design solution to any problems they encountered. They were given access to a variety of materials to aid the design process – for example PE equipment, such as bases for ball games, hoops, quoits, skipping ropes and a parachute, – as well as items of classroom furniture, plant pots and recyclable resources, such as cardboard boxes. The session proved to be a very creative experience, with children deeply involved in working through their ideas and finding solutions to the difficulties they faced. At the end of the session the groups shared their problems and solutions with everyone. Staff noted these comments and the children's ideas were incorporated into the final design plan for the playground. Afterwards the children returned to the classroom to record their thoughts and ideas through drawings and paintings.

Children at Victoria Road Primary School designing a new seating area. See Prompt sheet 3.5 and p. 67 for more information

Involving children in 'Thinking and planning'

Using models and plans

When to use this activity

Useful technique for:

- deciding where new features should be in the space;
- considering the impact of different layouts.

Preparation

Prepare a model or plan. This may be more meaningful to children if it is done in conjunction with them. Decide how to represent the planned features, for example small laminated images or symbolic objects.

Gathering the information

Children can position the representations of planned features in different places on the model or plan in response to questions such as
'Where would you like the quiet area/sandpit/ digging pit to be?'

Making sense of the information

Talk about the options with children as they participate. Consider capturing individual children's ideas through photographs for further review and discussion.

Issues to consider

Older children may be able to make sense of a two-dimensional plan of the space but younger children may find it easier to work with a three-dimensional model.

Consider using symbolic props with younger children or children who prefer to work directly in their outdoor space when thinking about these questions (see 'Getting started', Prompt sheet 2.2).

Involving children in 'Thinking and planning'

Developing ideas by visits to other developed outdoor environments

When to use this activity

Useful technique for:

- observing children's use of equipment and environments;
- widening children's experiences and awareness of potential solutions;
- gathering children's opinions;
- enabling children to make decisions based on a real experience;
- involving parents.

Preparation

As with any other visit off-site, careful attention must be given to preparation. Settings should follow the appropriate procedures before embarking on an off-site visit; for example, gaining parental permission, ensuring adequate staffing and completing a pre-visit risk assessment.

Ensure that the setting or place to be visited includes the type of features that are under consideration.

Consider how children's reactions, comments or views will be recorded during the visit. Options could include video or tape recorder, camera or notes.

Gathering the information

Observe children during the visit and discuss their experiences with them. Talk to the adults and children in the visited setting to gather their views about specific pieces of equipment.

Making sense of the information

Afterwards, provide opportunities to discuss the visit further, for example by encouraging children to record their thoughts through drawings and paintings. If photos have been taken, consider creating a display and offering children the chance to vote on their favourite experience during the visit (see Prompt sheet 3.4).

Issues to consider

The settings or places visited will need to be chosen carefully to ensure that the experiences that children have are a feasible option for their own environment.

Children using unfamiliar equipment for the first time may react to the experience differently to children who are familiar with it.

Involving children in 'Thinking and planning'

Recording information through 'mapping' activities

When to use this activity

Useful technique for:

- collating all the information gathered through earlier consultations with children, for example through tours of the space (see 'Getting started', Prompt sheet 2.1);
- providing a composite visual record of the places and spaces outdoors considered important by children;
- sharing children's perspectives with a wider audience, for example other children, parents, staff or management.

Preparation

Provide a large piece of paper and copies of materials generated by individual children during the initial consultations, for example their photographs and drawings from tours. Gather together additional resources such as pencils, crayons, paper and glue-sticks.

   (See Clark and Moss 2005: 39–43 for a detailed account of this technique in action.)

Gathering the information

Work with one or two children to make a 'map' of outdoors. Support the children to select the images and materials that they want to show on their map. Encourage them to add further information, for example by drawing or writing on the map. Offer to add captions of children's comments.

Making sense of the information

Ongoing conversations during the map-making activity will provide valuable insights into children's thoughts and priorities. The map-makers can be offered the opportunity to share their map with other children or staff. The finished maps can be displayed prominently to encourage further discussion.

Issues to consider

Some children may find it hard to relinquish 'their' photographs for a shared map-making activity. Consider providing each child with a set of their photographs to keep, and offer copies of all materials to be used for map-making.

Alison Clark working with
children at Happy Faces Preschool

Involving children in 'Thinking and planning'

Using photographs to identify priorities

When to use this activity

Useful technique for:

- identifying and ranking children's preferences and priorities across a range of options, for example seating, sandpit or growing area;
- identifying and ranking children's preferences for the options in relation to a specific feature, for example a raised/sunken/large/small sandpit;
- involving children in development of the vision plan.

Preparation

On the basis of the information gathered from everyone, make up a set of photographs that show the options for development, for example a sandpit, a gardening area, seating or playhouse.

Or make up a set of photographs that show a variety of options for a specific feature, such as various types of seating.

Draw up a chart to record children's preferences and priorities.

Gathering the information

Show individual children two photographs at a time and ask them to decide which is the best/most important.

Record the favoured option on the chart and continue for all pairs.

Making sense of the information

Count the number of times an option has been favoured and place all the options in a rank order, for example:

Ranking different features		*Ranking the options for one feature*	
Sandpit	4	Large sandpit	4
Growing area	3	Sunken sandpit	3
Playhouse	2	Raised sandpit	2
Seating	1	Small sandpit	1

Issues to consider

Avoid overwhelming children with too many decisions.
Make sure that the options shown to children are feasible and under real consideration.

Involving children in 'Thinking and planning'

Developing designs

When to use this activity

Useful technique for:

- solving design problems;
- overcoming potential conflicts in the layout of features or equipment;
- checking the impact of different features in the space;
- active children who prefer to work in a space rather than with representational materials.

Preparation

Assemble a collection of objects and materials that can be used by children to symbolise a feature or to mark out an area; for example, carpet tiles, skipping ropes, lining paper, bamboo canes, blankets, hoops, cones, plastic bricks or cardboard boxes. Remember, anything can be used to represent anything!

Gathering the information

Work with small groups of children to achieve the aim of the session. For example, the purpose may be to decide the position and size of a new sandpit, or to work out a route around the garden for wheeled toys, or to consider the impact of allocating part of the garden to children under two years old or to work out the design of seating. Encourage children to use the materials provided to work through the design issues and help them to think through and resolve any ensuing problems. For example, children may decide that potted plants growing along a fence will improve the look of the fence and stop balls rolling under it, but will the gate still open?

Making sense of the information

Use a camera to capture the stages of children's thinking and the different ideas and designs that are tried out before the final solution is found. Once developed, these photographs provide a valuable record of the session as well as providing useful material for displays or a book, to prompt further discussion. A 3-D model that shows children's final designs is a very good way to reaffirm the ideas that have been developed and share them with a wider audience.

Issues to consider

Some children become despondent very quickly if their initial idea is found to have 'flaws'. Support children to see the session as a positive problem-solving process and encourage them to think of ways to adapt their ideas and try again.

Page 67 shows children at Victoria Road Primary School designing their new seating area.

Victoria Road Primary School, Ashford

See Case study 3.2, p. 60 for further information.

Children deciding on the design for their new seating area

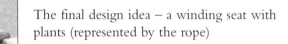

The final design idea – a winding seat with plants (represented by the rope)

The new seating area

4 Making it happen

Developing an implementation plan

Once the vision plan has been produced, the use of each area has been decided upon and the potential solutions have been identified, the implementation or action plan needs to be developed. This sets out the steps and stages for turning the development plans for outdoors into a reality.

In preparing the implementation plan there are a number of issues to record:

- the specific elements of the project;
- timescale and order of proceeding;
- who will do the work;
- whether specialist advice is needed;
- how children will be involved;
- types of materials required;
- any technical and legal requirements;
- contact details and quotations from suppliers and contractors;
- costs;
- funding sources;
- completion target date.

The plan helps sort out and keep track of the tasks to be accomplished. It also provides a project record that may be a useful support to funding applications (see Figures 4.1 and 4.2).

Several settings successfully involved families, the local community and businesses in the implementation of their plans. By seeking donations and making good use of volunteer support precious funds can be preserved for services and materials that must be paid for.

Children at Glebe House Day Nursery helping to plant donated apple trees

Case study 4.1 Involving others to 'make it happen': Bertie's Playgroup

Bertie's Playgroup uses a classroom at Ethelbert Road Infant School. They have sole use of a fenced area of the playground just outside the classroom. Staff and children make good use of their outdoor area but recognise that it could be improved. A clear vision plan was formed, based on their consultations with staff, parents and children. One of the emerging priorities for outdoors was improved storage that was accessible to children. The outdoor area was surveyed to identify the best site for a new storage facility and it became apparent that a large raised flowerbed would need to be removed.

To keep costs to a minimum a decision was made to appeal for help in breaking up and removing the bed. A letter and notice to parents resulted in offers of labour and tools, staff also volunteered to help. The date was set, the skip was ordered, and one sunny Saturday morning the volunteers assembled at school to accomplish their task.

Several back-breaking hours later, the skip was full and the area was cleared and ready to be prepared for the shed base. The collection of the skip from the school playground on Monday was an unexpected highlight for the children, who were able to watch it being lifted and taken away.

The rest of this chapter features a selection of illustrative case studies that explore how some of the most common issues faced by early years practitioners were overcome through the project in Kent. The prompt sheets at the end of the chapter give details of some of the ways that children were involved in 'making it happen' in their outdoor space.

The imagination and creativity shown by practitioners and project teams in seeking and identifying solutions is an inspiration and shows that, with determination, even the most challenging problems can be significantly reduced, or completely overcome.

Task	Who will lead?	Timescales	Useful contacts	Who will carry out the work?	How will children be involved?	Materials needed	Technical or legal issues	Costs	Funding source	Completion target date

Remember to keep a record of all the consultation and activity work you have completed with the children, as this can often provide important information for funders when applying for financial support with a project.

Figure 4.1 Example of an implementation plan

Barrier to improving outdoor play	Action	Involvement of Children	Responsibility	Resources	Cost	Timescale	Monitoring progress – how and who	Evaluating success
Lack of safety surface	Get two or three quotes for safety surface / Install safety surface		Sheila	Supplied by contractor	To be confirmed	End of March	Sheila to send Gail quotes	Safety surface down by end of April
No provision for children to explore sounds	Get hold of unwanted saucepans etc. / Create sound area – on railings	Decorate saucepans	Sheila to co-ordinate efforts of staff team/parents etc.	Time – hunting at jumble sales and car boot sales etc.	£20?	End of March	Sheila to keep Gail informed Saucepans in situ by end of March Send Gail photos	Children able to explore sounds outside
No provision for children to draw outdoors	Provide blackboards attached to shed	Can help identify position on shed – right height	Staff team	Time – preparing and painting boards	£30?	End of March	Sheila to keep Gail informed Blackboards in situ by end of March Send Gail photos	Children able to draw outside
Lack of surface for bikes and wheeled toys	Identify minimum width needed to enable children to ride bikes and pass each other / Work out a scale plan for the cycle track and position of pebble roundabout / Visit local example of pebbles with children	Children to paint pebbles	Sheila: Co-ordinate visit with Mark / Staff to plan for painting sessions with children	Paving slabs Cement / Volunteer help?	To be confirmed Send Gail two or three estimates re the cost of extending the cycle track	End of April	Sheila to keep Gail informed Let Gail know dates of visit re pebbles Send Gail a scale drawing of proposed cycle track Take photos of the children painting their pebble	Cycle track and pebble round about in place by end of April / Children using track after Easter holidays
No provision for children to care for plants/ observe seasonal changes in their environment	Develop raised flower bed	Fill bed with earth	Sheila with help from Paul Boyce (the garden gate)	Planting seeds and plants	To be confirmed Send Gail two or three estimates re the cost	End of March ? in time for planting	Sheila to keep Gail informed of progress Take photos	Children able to plant after Easter holidays
No provision for sand play	Provide a sandpit – sunken to ensure access by SEN child / Identify best size and position for new sandpit	Discuss and trial position using temporary sandpit	Sheila		To be confirmed Send Gail two or three estimates	By beginning of Summer term	Sheila to keep Gail informed of progress Take photos	Children using sandpit by May half term

Figure 4.2 Draft action plan, MCMA Preschool

Case study 4.2 **Involving others to 'make it happen': Highways at Hamstreet Kindergarten**

This setting enlisted the help of families, the school and businesses in the community to implement their plans for the garden. They held a very successful 'Groundforce Day' and invited children and parents to come and help with a variety of tasks, such as fencing, painting, path laying and weaving. The provision of soup and rolls gave everyone a break at lunchtime and the energy to carry on afterwards.

The kindergarten also participated in an activity week organised in conjunction with the adjoining school. During the week children and staff worked hard to transform their recently erected pergola into a spectacular sensory experience

The staff also had significant success in attracting donations and gifts from businesses in their local community. The local golf clubs gave unwanted balls, the local garden centre donated some 'end-of-line' pots and planters. The supervisor attributes their success to having an upfront attitude towards asking people and being able to give potential donors a clear message about the importance of what they were trying to achieve and the significant benefit to children from the donations.

Case study 4.3 Involvement and support from business: Bell Wood Community Primary School

Learning through Landscapes, in partnership with electricity supplier EDF Energy, runs an annual award scheme to recognise and reward good practice outdoors in school grounds. EDF Energy also offers their employees the opportunity to take part in a 'Team Challenge Day'. Each team volunteers their labour for a day, and they have a small budget to provide some materials.

Bell Wood Community Primary School were an ideal candidate for a 'Team Challenge'. The school were working hard to make their plans to turn land that was an underused eyesore into a haven for wildlife. The work had begun but progress was slow and other priorities within the school were taking precedence. Consequently, key personnel involved in the project were becoming anxious at the lack of momentum. The EDF Energy team took up the challenge to finish the fencing, help with planting the wildlife garden, and replant the flowerbed at the school entrance. The day was a great success and the school were thrilled with the progress that had been made in such a short time. It gave staff and children renewed impetus and enthusiasm to finish the wildlife garden and start using it.

Finding solutions to management and organisational issues

Case study 4.4 Carrying out a risk assessment before introducing free-flow access to outdoors: Sunshine and Showers Nursery

The staff at Sunshine and Showers Nursery were keen to introduce free-flow access to outdoors and planned to provide an environment that offered children risk and challenge. However, they recognised that a free-flow system would have implications for staffing levels both indoors and outdoors and therefore needed to be carefully planned and implemented to ensure that levels of safety were maintained. As part of their preparations for introducing the new system they carried out a risk assessment on their outdoor space. The staff recognised that parents would each have a unique and valuable perspective on the potential risks for their own child so they invited parents to be involved in the initial assessment.

After an information session to outline the nursery's plans for developing the outdoor space, parents were given an opportunity to tour the garden with staff and identify any areas or features that they felt would give rise to an unacceptable risk for their child. The collaborative session with parents was constructive and purposeful, and parental worries were noted. Further meetings were held to allow staff to voice their concerns. The Accident Record Book provided another source of information for analysis by staff. After all the information had been gathered and reviewed, the plans for the garden progressed smoothly and free-flow access was introduced with full parental support. The staff continue to review their procedures, consult with parents and analyse the Accident Book to ensure that children benefit from the natural challenges that the garden offers, such as climbing in the bushes, while being protected from unacceptable levels of risk.

See the Bibliography for details of a publication that promotes the importance of risk and challenge in young children's lives, *Too Safe for Their Own Good,* by Jennie Lindon.

Case study 4.5 **Introducing free-flow access to outdoors: Happy Faces Preschool**

The preschool children had direct access to an enclosed outdoor space yet were only able to use it at prescribed times during the day. As the project progressed staff recognised the need to increase children's opportunities to be outdoors. However, they had to overcome several organisational issues in order to implement a new system that allowed children to flow freely between the indoor and outdoor environments. Below is a summary of the issues and concerns debated by staff. The solutions that they found indicate that a positive and creative problem-solving attitude works wonders, and has a positive impact on the provision being made both indoors and outdoors.

Issue	Suggestion	Advantages	Concerns	Solutions	Impact
Access route	Use the fire door at the rear of one classroom	Direct route	Classroom becoming cold as children entered and left	Reorganise use of space in hallway and use double doors next to cloakroom area	Improved access direct from hall and cloakroom area Classroom remains warm
Children's management of coats and wellies	Encourage children towards independence	Children develop useful skills Not dependent on adult help	Children not properly protected from extreme weather conditions Cloakroom area untidy	Trial period introduced to see how the system would work	Most children quickly learnt to manage their outdoor clothes themselves. Staff reassured. Minimal support given to a few children that needed it
Staff deployment and maintaining ratios	Staff to be deployed to work in designated areas, including outdoors	Staff clear about roles and responsibilities Children have adult support outdoors	Ratios not maintained since staff not always responding to the variations in numbers as children flow between indoors and outdoors	Discussion among staff team to ensure that all felt confident and able to use their initiative and redeploy themselves indoors/ outdoors should the need arise	Staff more confident and move freely between indoors and outdoors as necessary. Staff able to give better support to children as their play develops

Case study 4.6 Overcoming staff reservations about introducing free-flow access to outdoors: Highways at Hamstreet Kindergarten

Very early on in the Space to Grow project the staff at Highways at Hamstreet Kindergarten were already supporting children to make good use of outdoors for a significant part of both the morning and afternoon sessions. They had overcome all initial hurdles, such as identifying an independent access route, ensuring that the garden was securely fenced, the development of good resources, the provision of suitable clothing and wellies and engaging the support of parents. However, puzzlingly, they had not yet taken the final step of introducing 'free-flow' access.

Discussion with the supervisor revealed a deep-rooted anxiety about maintaining children's safety outdoors in the garden under a free-flow system. Interestingly, this stance was at odds with her general attitude towards outdoor play, which was positive and acknowledged the importance of children experiencing risk and challenge in their lives. Further probing revealed that her concern was very specific: how to keep children safe when the garden was adjacent to a busy road with only a single gate in-between. This worry was exacerbated by other adults using the gate to enter the kindergarten at unspecified times.

The solution was a combination of common sense and discussion among staff and with parents, combined with the introduction of a system of sensible precautions to minimise the risk of a child inadvertently slipping through the gate. To her credit the supervisor overcame her own high level of anxiety in order to lead the staff towards resolving this issue. In a subsequent review all staff recognised that the introduction of a free-flow system had been a resounding success.

Case study 4.7 Free-flow access – keeping children safe in summer: Bright Beginnings Day Nursery

The staff and children moved into their brand-new building in September 2003. The beginning of the Space to Grow project coincided with this move and provided a catalyst for developing the outdoor environment from the remains of a building site into a stimulating place for play and learning. An initial decision was made to focus on familiarising children with the indoor environment for the first few months, and to begin consultations about the development of outdoors in the spring term.

The plans for outdoors progressed well and by the summer term staff and children were enjoying periods of free-flow access to outdoors throughout the day. However, the summer months revealed a problem; a lack of shade over much of the play area. This naturally gave rise to discussions about the importance of keeping children safe in the sun and staff identified the need to devise a system whereby children were protected without losing their free access to outdoors.

First, parents were requested to supply sun cream and ensure their child was protected on arrival at nursery. Permission was also sought from parents to allow staff to reapply sun cream as necessary. The next stage involved stationing a member of staff under the large covered veranda area just outside the exit doors, to ensure that the first time each child chose to go outside sun cream was applied and a note made of the time. The combination of sun cream, sun hats and covering up, coupled with an emphasis on activities under the veranda on particularly hot days, kept children safe and protected and enabled them to continue to benefit from their outdoor area.

Case study 4.8 Introducing free-flow access in a Reception class: Mongeham Primary School:

The two Reception classes at Mongeham Primary School shared use of an enclosed outdoor area and staff valued the opportunities that outdoor play offers. However, they recognised the need for a system for monitoring and managing children's use of the space.

The indoor classroom was already organised to allow children to select the activities they wished to engage in, through a 'peg and picture' system. This system gave children choice and independence but let staff predetermine the number of children at any one activity. Children quickly learnt that if there was no space for their peg they would need to find an alternative. Initially this system was extended to give children an opportunity to choose 'outdoor toys' by placing their peg on the corresponding picture and going outside. Once this routine had been successfully established staff refined it further by providing pictures of different outdoor resources and experiences. This acted as a catalyst for children's play and also ensured that the numbers of children using specific pieces of equipment did not constitute a safety hazard.

By putting in place effective systems that gave children independence in both the indoor and outdoor environments staff were relieved of patrolling and head-counting duties and were able to focus on supporting children's play and learning.

Case study 4.9 **Improving children's access to outdoors: Saplings @ The Sports Centre**

Saplings @ The Sports Centre is accommodated in an upstairs room within the sports centre. The nursery management have negotiated use of a piece of land behind the centre to enable children and staff to access outdoors. However, the route to this outdoor area is via stairs, corridors, doors and locked gates, so allowing children independent access is not a feasible option. Discussion with staff revealed further issues to be overcome: ensuring the security of equipment and the practicalities of resourcing and setting up an outdoor area so far away from the indoor environment. Despite these difficulties the day nursery staff were

enthusiastic about outdoors. They were eager to find a way of developing the area and giving children a significant amount of time in it. Their determination and persistence paid off and a practical solution was eventually identified – the creation of an 'outdoor classroom'. The project award enabled the day nursery to purchase a large secure storage shed with wide doors. The shed was organised and equipped to allow children to independently access and return the resources they needed for their play.

This option addressed all the identified issues: it reduced concerns about security, it minimised the amount of 'setting up' needed and it allowed resources and equipment to be stored permanently within the outdoor area, rather than being transported there on a daily basis by staff. The staff are very pleased with the progress that has been made and the creation of an 'outdoor classroom' has provided a good starting point for further development and use of the space.

Case study 4.10 **Overcoming a lack of space: Pipsqueaks Day Nursery**

Pipsqueaks Day Nursery is a privately owned and recently established day nursery on the Isle of Sheppey. The day nursery has very limited outdoor space on-site, little more than an alley. The staff recognise the importance of children accessing outdoors and regularly take the children to a local memorial park. The focus of the developments at Pipsqueaks Day Nursery has been to enrich children's learning experiences in the local public spaces and to improve the outdoor learning on-site. Having observed what children liked to do both indoors and at the local park, the staff used this information to inform their development plans. The two key issues were to find ways to make best use of the limited space on-site and to improve children's play and learning experiences in the park.

An initial review of the access in and out of the nursery indicated that, with some minor adjustments, children could be given free-flow access to the alley from the rear of the building. This immediately increased the amount of time that they could spend outside and took pressure off the space since not all children accessed it simultaneously. Staff have also made imaginative use of the vertical wall space to maximise children's experiences and opportunities for learning. For example, oven racks and crepe paper offer children chances to weave and develop co-ordination of hand and eye movements. Using brushes to 'paint' different surfaces with water provides children with opportunities to observe changes to materials; for example, as the wall-mounted slate tiles turn from being dull grey to shiny black. A shelf unit against one wall is used to store small boxes of equipment for children to access and choose from during the session. Netting and old CDs suspended above children's heads create extra interest without using up valuable floor space. To improve the provision being made in the park, staff have collected a range of resources that are multi-functional and lightweight. For example, younger children use a clothes airer and some lengths of material to make dens, but older children also use the airer with pegs for mathematical sorting opportunities. Balls and hoops support physical development. Washing-up bowls are used as stepping stones and for imaginative games. Each day children are involved in choosing what is transported on a trolley to the park. The box of musical instruments is a popular choice, and children also like re-enacting favourite stories, such as 'We're Going on a Bear Hunt'.

Sharing outdoor space: St John's Primary School and Preschool

The Reception children at St John's Primary School share their outdoor space with the committee-run preschool in the adjoining classroom. The two staff teams have worked together to identify their joint and individual priorities for developing the space. There have been many issues to resolve and hurdles to overcome and some are still under discussion. The table below highlights some of the key dilemmas faced by the staff, as well as some of the potential solutions.

Issue	Staff concerns	Potential solutions	Advantages
Responsibility for setting up and tidying away the outdoor area	For organisational reasons, specific tasks will be carried out by one team rather than shared by both	Ensure that equipment is stored in low-level labelled units	Children can select and return equipment themselves No need for either staff team to 'set up' or tidy away outdoor area
Deployment of staff	Both staff teams have several areas to supervise, both indoors and outdoors Because each team works under different management systems and has to conform to different regulations it is not possible to share responsibility for staffing outdoors	Consider staff deployment as separate teams, to allow each team to find own solutions. Then look at the two solutions together to see how they would work in tandem outdoors	Enables each staff team to meet their different statutory regulations regarding ratios

Issue	Staff concerns	Potential solutions	Advantages
Use of equipment and resources by different age groups (two–five years)	The two staff teams work with children who may have up to a three-year difference in age Not all equipment is suitable for children at either end of this age spectrum	Jointly evaluate all existing equipment and consider its suitability for the full age range Consider the full age range of children when adding new equipment to the area Identify the purpose of different pieces of equipment and consider how older/younger children might use them Label and organise storage to ensure that specific pieces of equipment that are really only appropriate for under-threes or over-fives are only accessible to these children Discuss storage and organisation with children and develop a shared and understood system for the use of different items, for example: • items in the blue cupboard are only to be used by two-year-olds • items in the red cupboard must be used with an adult	Most equipment will be suitable for all children – although they may well use it in different ways Both staff teams and all children have been involved in developing and implementing the system, therefore the system is more likely to be adhered to by all A small range of specific items of equipment is protected from inappropriate use by older/younger children

Issue	Staff concerns	Potential solutions	Advantages
Long-term maintenance of the area and seasonal replacement of resources, for example sand, seeds	How to share out the cost and responsibility for the replacement and replenishment of outdoor items	Review the existing system: ● discuss the existing roles and responsibilities among both staff teams, senior management and grounds maintenance staff ● identify current levels of expenditure on maintaining the outdoor space ● identify which budgets are currently being used Consider creating a shared budget that is contributed to by both the preschool and the primary school Use this fund to cover ongoing expenditure and maintenance costs Agree any changes to the roles and responsibilities of existing grounds maintenance staff	The creation of a shared budget will ensure that future expenditure on the garden can be financed and will provide for the longer-term maintenance of the shared space

Case study 4.12 **Developing outdoor provision despite an uncertain future: Mary Sheridan Preschool**

Mary Sheridan Preschool is situated on premises with a large garden and it provides for children with special educational needs. When the preschool originally joined the project the aim was to develop the large garden. However, it became apparent that the preschool's future in their current premises was uncertain, and that at some point relocation to a different building was very likely.

Having established children's enthusiasms and interests, the preschool staff reviewed their original plans and after some discussion the new plans focused on:

- developing the small courtyard immediately outside the classroom;
- improving children's independent access to the courtyard;
- improving outdoor experiences for less mobile children;
- protecting children from wet and damp conditions;
- acquisition of resources and equipment that could be easily moved to new premises.

Case study 4.13 **Developing outdoor provision despite an uncertain future: St Martin's Preschool Group**

St Martin's Preschool Group are a long-established setting based in a church hall with good access to an outdoor area. In recent years the garden has benefited from some improvements, for example a new surface for wheeled toys. The preschool joined the project with the aim of making further improvements and structural changes to the garden. Sadly, a significant drop in numbers of children attending has made the long-term viability of the preschool very uncertain. This situation also makes expensive structural changes in the garden a potential waste of  time, money and effort. So the staff and committee have been forced to rethink their plans for outdoors.

However, rather than do nothing at all, the preschool has chosen to concentrate their energy and funds into developing a series of resource boxes for supporting outdoor learning. Some boxes will be developed to further support the kinds of experience that staff know children currently enjoy, for example gardening and investigating. Other boxes will be put together to support outdoor opportunities that staff feel children are not currently experiencing to full advantage, for example den-building and exploration of different weather conditions.

The advantage of this solution is that in the short term children and staff can make better use of their existing outdoor environment, while in the longer term, should the preschool no longer be viable, the resource boxes can be reallocated to other local preschools.

Meeting training needs

Case study 4.14 In-service training for staff: Ditton Church Preschool

Having officially opened their garden in May, the staff at Ditton Church Preschool realised that they would benefit from further help in developing their role in supporting children's learning outdoors. Consequently, they were quick to respond to the offer of a free workshop advertised in the Space to Grow project newsletter.

Outdoor play workshops

The Kent Space to Grow project aims to help settings develop more than just the physical outdoor space. As we all recognise, even a well-resourced environment is not going to be fully effective as a place for children to play and learn without enthusiastic knowledgeable staff who can support the process. The review meetings revealed that for some settings, lower levels of staff motivation for outdoor play are linked to a lack of confidence in their own role as outdoor educators, as well as uncertainty about ways to promote and support different learning experiences outdoors. If this strikes a chord...then read on!

What is in the back of your storage shed?
Do the children know it is there?
How often is it used?

I am setting aside two weeks from **14–25th June** to provide a **FREE WORKSHOP on Outdoor Play** to any project setting who requests one. I can be flexible about timing, morning? afternoon? twilight? – even over the weekend! You just have to get everyone there! I am happy to tailor each two-hour workshop to your own requirements. Do you need specific curriculum ideas, for example about supporting mathematical learning outdoors? Or do you need a more general session about the adult role? What about a close look at your existing equipment to identify new ways of using it and to pinpoint any gaps in your resources? Or would it be helpful to see some images showing provision in other settings for discussion and inspiration...?

If you are interested, please call me to book a date and discuss your training needs.

An informal observation of staff outdoors and a chat with the supervisor indicated the usefulness of a workshop focusing on the staff's role, the curriculum, safety issues and the development of a shared understanding about codes of behaviour. The workshop took place outdoors one afternoon and the tasks and activities concentrated on a number of discussion points.

Staff role

Staff were asked to:

- think about their role indoors;
- identify the kind of demands children made on them as individuals;
- identify the kind of interaction that was taking place between adults and children.

Their responses were shared within the workshop session to identify any similarities and differences between the role of adults indoors and outdoors, as a starting point for further discussion.

To promote further discussion staff were asked to discuss a proforma published in *Playing Outside* (Bilton 2004) that identifies the type of demands made by children outdoors.

Next staff were asked to:

- identify the types of demand they dealt with dealt with most outdoors;
- consider any emerging trends or patterns; for example, why some staff always take children to the toilet, or others tend to be deployed at sedentary activities;
- identify any changes that need to be made to develop their role as outdoor educators;
- begin to think about how to achieve these changes.

Equipment and curriculum issues

Staff were asked to:

- review the current provision outdoors;
- identify any gaps in the existing provision.

Outcomes of the discussion:

- no need to replicate exactly the provision indoors and outdoors;
- aim to provide different experiences with same aims/opportunities for learning, e.g. drawing table inside, large-scale painting outside;
- use outdoors to provide experiences that are harder to offer indoors.

Next, staff were asked to:

- work in pairs and use books relating to outdoor play experiences to identify potential activities to address gaps in existing provision;
- share lists of ideas and resources with the staff team;
- identify some key resources.

Safety and codes for behaviour

Staff were asked to:

- discuss and identify key issues and their concerns regarding safety;
- consider the benefits to children of experiencing risk and challenge outdoors.

Outcomes of the discussion:

- staff planned to discuss 'codes for behaviour' outdoors with children;
- involve children in developing these codes;
- ensure a shared understanding of what these codes mean in practice;
- staff aim to share reminders about codes in a positive way, i.e. 'we always walk with tools' rather than 'don't run with tools'; 'we always turn the tap off' rather than 'don't waste water'.

The staff at Ditton Church Preschool valued the opportunity to discuss these issues and develop a shared understanding of their role as outdoor educators, and their provision and practice outdoors has moved forward as a direct consequence of this training session.

Developing resources

Case study 4.15 **Improving the storage and organisation of resources: White Oak Preschool**

White Oak Preschool has a secure accessible garden and both staff and children make good use of it throughout the year. Children are able to take indoor equipment outside to develop their play ideas. However, staff recognised that if the outdoor storage facilities were reorganised and improved a wider range of materials and resources could be provided in the garden to enrich children's outdoor experiences. The acquisition of a large shed with wide double doors has enabled them to achieve this aim. Equipment is stored inside in labelled boxes. Staff agree that the impact of these changes has been very positive:

- children can independently choose and return the materials they need;
- the range of outdoor resources has been expanded;
- there is enriched potential for outdoor experiences;
- there is no conflict of use between children wanting to use resources, such as the tea set, indoors and those who wish to take the same item outdoors.

Developing design solutions

Case study 4.16 Improving children's access to a pond and bog garden: Northfleet Nursery School

Northfleet Nursery School is a maintained nursery in North Kent near Gravesend. It has been established for many years and the staff and children make very good use of the outdoor environment for play and learning across all areas of the curriculum. The focus of their developments as part of the Space to Grow project was the redesign of a small sunken pond and bog garden. In previous years this feature had been a well-used and important resource; however, a decision was taken to prevent children accessing it following the arrival of a child at the nursery who was unable to recognise the difference between types of surface, i.e. tarmac, grass or water. Consequently, he regularly got wet trying to run across the pond, and had great difficulty understanding the potential hazard in this part of the garden.

   Staff recognised that in the longer term a design solution had to be found that allowed for access to the pond for all children. Having cleared the area around the original pond and researched various options with the children, the final solution was the design and installation of a raised pond and bog garden with decked access from all sides. The improved access allowed more children to use the area simultaneously, while the raised design minimised the likelihood of children falling into the water.

Case study 4.17 **Overcoming environmental problems: Happy Faces Preschool**

Staff and children at Happy Faces Preschool were already making good use of one part of their large outdoor area. However, the remaining space was undeveloped because the land was affected by an underground spring, resulting in extremely boggy conditions throughout the year. The challenge was to find a way of overcoming this problem and allowing children use of the rest of the garden.

Through the determined efforts of a small group of parents the area was slowly transformed. A willow tunnel and moisture-loving plants were planted to absorb some of the excess water in the soil. A sensory arbour was built with seating and a solar-powered fountain. To allow children to cross and use the boggiest part of the garden, a raised timber decking structure was created in the form of lily pads linked by a bridge.

Involving children in 'Making it happen'

Growing and planting

Preparation

Gather together the tools and resources you will need, for example trowels, pots, plants, seeds, seedlings, watering cans and aprons.

Share stories and factual information about the care of plants with children.

Make labels for plants: laminate children's drawings and writing and attach to lollipop sticks.

Issues to consider

Be attentive to hygiene issues and ensure that children are able to wash their hands after handling soil.

Involve children in the ongoing care of plants and seedlings, for example watering and weeding routines.

Involving children in 'Making it happen'

Creating a sensory area

Preparation

Gather together the resources you will need. Recycle and re-use! Be creative! Local 'scrap schemes' can be a very good source of suitable items.

Consider using:

strips of plastic	twigs and branches
beads	string, wool, rope
CDs	shells
feathers	ribbons
garden netting	plastic bottles
scraps of material	foil food trays.

Issues to consider

The weather will take its toll on children's creations, however, this can be a very good reason for renewing and revitalising the sensory area with new materials at a later date, with a different intake of children.

Involving children in 'Making it happen'

Weaving on fences

Preparation

Gather together the resources you will need. For example, lengths of material, strips of sacking, rope, plastic, barrier tape, grasses, feathers, sticks and twigs.

Issues to consider

The weather will take its toll on children's woven creations, however, this can be a very good reason for renewing and revitalising the fence with new weaving.

Large areas of fencing will take time to complete; consider working on it for short periods over a week. Volunteer help from parents can provide invaluable extra support for the weaving project.

Involving children in 'Making it happen'

Painting murals

Preparation

Gather together the resources and materials you will need; for example, paints, brushes, protective clothing for adults and children.

  Have fun!

Issues to consider

You may want to seal children's work afterwards with a varnish to give it a longer-lasting finish.

5 Evaluating and enjoying

Monitor and evaluate the changes outdoors

At each stage of the project it is important to evaluate the progress that has been made.

- Have the changes improved the outdoor environment?
- Is it being used in the way that was originally intended? If not, why not?

In Ditton Church Preschool the ongoing review by staff and children resulted in adaptations to some of the initial plans. For example, children and staff had originally identified planting opportunities as a priority; however, once the two donated planters were in situ it became clear that children valued them as a base for imaginative play. After discussion the plans were changed to allow one planter to be developed as a catalyst for imaginative play. Case study 5.1 outlines further changes that were made at the preschool following an evaluation once the garden was in full use.

Case study 5.1 Reviewing the use of the garden at Ditton Church Preschool

Having officially opened their new garden at the beginning of May, the staff and children were thoroughly enjoying using it during the summer term. However, after a few weeks it became apparent that some features were not being used in the way that was originally intended and others were not being used much at all. The staff decided to spend time reviewing the children's use of the garden and this review highlighted the following issues:

- the bark pit was rarely used;
- the digging pit was so popular that staff and parents were having trouble keeping up with the laundering of muddy clothes;
- children were using the shingle path as a source of transportable materials for their trucks, and the presence of shingle all over the grass was making it hard to cut;
- the storage and retrieval of wellies was disorganised – staff and children were spending too long looking for a matching pair.

Following the review the garden was reorganised to take account of these issues:

- the bark pit was replaced with earth;
- the shingle path was replaced with the bark and a new area was created where children could play with shingle;

- the flowers in the free-standing planter were repositioned against the fence on the site of the original bark and digging pits;
- the earth in the planter was made available to children for digging;
- the welly storage under the bench was replaced with a transparent storage system that enabled boots to be stored in pairs and easily visible to whoever was searching for a particular set.

This new arrangement in the garden ensured that children still had the same opportunities outdoors but that the management of these experiences was improved.

Aim to involve the whole setting community in evaluating the changes to the outdoor area. There are lots of ways to do this.

- Invite parents in to see the improvements for themselves.
- Encourage children to take their parents on a tour of their favourite places and activities. For more ideas to involve children in evaluating the changes see the Prompt sheets at the end of this chapter.
- Hold events outdoors so that everyone gets a chance to explore the space and comment on the developments that have taken place.
- Put up displays that show the outdoor area changing over time. At Ditton Church Preschool the project team made a video of their efforts to transform their outdoor area, and it was shown to guests at the event to open the garden.

- Show photographs of children engrossed in outdoor play and display captions alongside each photograph indicating what the children were interested in, what they were saying and doing, and how their play progressed.
- Invite members of the management team to come and see how the space has changed, and talk to staff and children about the new opportunities being provided.

It is easier to maintain enthusiasm for outdoors if everyone can see the types of experience children have, and how they respond to their new outdoor environment. Why not arrange for parents to drop off or collect children from an active outdoor session, rather than from indoors? This will also give the opportunity for parents to observe children playing and for staff to relate the experiences that individual children have been interested and involved in.

Sustain and maintain

Having spent so much time, energy and money improving the outdoor space it is crucial to plan for its sustainability in the longer term. To ensure that it continues to be developed it is essential to think about the maintenance and upkeep of the space and include these costs in the annual budget.

It will also be necessary to discuss and decide upon roles and responsibilities for the area within the staff and management team and, if applicable, among other users.

Consider the following issues.

- Who will carry out safety checks?
- Who will be responsible for ordering replacement items or seasonal items?
- Who will maintain the fences and boundaries to ensure children's safety?
- Have the changes outdoors altered or increased the responsibilities of those staff already involved with its upkeep and maintenance?
- If so, has this been accounted for through a review of the existing job description or maintenance contract?
- How can the children be involved in the care and upkeep of the outdoor space?
- How will organisation, routines and codes of behaviour for outdoors be developed and shared among staff and children?

Enjoying – celebrating success

Whenever an element of the plan has been successfully implemented make sure everyone is aware of the achievement, however large or small. Marking each phase of the project shows the setting community that progress has been made; it also acknowledges the hard work that has been undertaken and it motivates everyone to make more effort and move forward towards the next stage.

There are lots of ways to share what has been achieved at each stage.

Unused alley at Pipsqueaks Day Nursery 'before' the project

- Put up posters.
- Send out a newsletter.
- Organise a display of 'before' and 'after' photographs.
- Display children's drawings of the developments alongside captions of their comments.
- Display photographs of children using the new area.

The development of the outdoor space, and the involvement of everyone in that process, is a big accomplishment. Children, their families, staff and the local community will feel the positive benefits of the improvements that have been achieved. So, mark the end of the project with a big celebration.

Using CDs to improve the look of alley at
Pipsqueaks Day Nursery

Children and staff at Pipsqueaks Day Nursery
now making good use of the alley

- Organise an event for children and their families.
- Invite a local dignitary to officially open the newly
  developed space.
- Invite representatives from sponsoring organisations or
  award bodies.
- Invite the local press.

Postman Pat and the local MP opening the garden at
Ditton Church Preschool

The Mayor of Tonbridge at Happy Faces Preschool   The EDF Energy Team Challenge at Bell Wood Community Primary School

What happened next?

In July 2005 the Kent Space to Grow project reached the final stages. The twenty-two settings involved had moved a long way towards achieving the key aims of the project; to improve children's access to and use of outdoors, to enhance the quality of children's experiences outdoors, and to increase practitioner confidence, motivation and enthusiasm for outdoor learning. The practitioners were asked to evaluate what they had learnt through their participation, and identify what they would do differently another time. Figure 5.1 highlights these comments and will be of significant interest to anyone considering a similar undertaking.

The project was full of challenges and obstacles that were met with determination and persistence by the settings involved. Their hard work paid off and as the project drew to a close many settings also noted the positive impact that changing and developing the use of the outdoor learning environment had on their indoor environment. Staff reported lower levels of noise indoors, higher levels of concentration and calmer more purposeful play amongst children. Similarly, having discovered that learning outdoors can be successfully supported through activities that are initiated and led by children, some practitioners began to question whether a similar approach could be used indoors. Consequently, several settings moved away from plans that were based round a topic or theme and embraced a planning approach that has the child at its centre and uses children's current interests and enthusiasms to provide direction and focus for the interaction, resources and experiences that are offered.

What have you learnt?	What would you do differently?
• Children have a lot to offer us – ideas, enthusiasm • The project has strengthened bonds between staff and parents. • The use of outdoors changes the use of indoors • Outdoors has a positive impact on learning and children's behaviour • Networking with others is vital • Involving others is essential • To start from what you have and develop it • To seek donations – don't be embarrassed to ask for what you want	• Plan project thoroughly – don't rush in • Manage time spent on the project carefully • Delegate • Look for ways to combine initiatives and work together • Tell people informed throughout the project • Use knowledge and observation of children to inform the project • Involve children throughout the project • Take account of seasonal factors when planning the outdoor space • Give external contractors a very specific brief and closely supervise their work • Record the process – for funding bids, external regulatory bodies

Figure 5.1 Evaluating what has been learnt

Involving children in 'Evaluating and enjoying'

Surveying the existing space: tours (see Clark and Moss 2005: 37–9)

When to use this activity

Useful technique for:

- active children who like to be on the move;
- identifying emerging favourite spaces;
- surveying new or changed features in the environment;
- identifying new features, items or activities of importance to the child;
- reviewing the space before and after any developments (see 'Getting started', Prompt sheet 2.1).

Use this activity to review and build up information about what children like to do outdoors following the implementation of the planned changes.

Preparation and resources

Offer children a variety of methods for recording their views during the tour. Options could include:

- cameras;
- clipboards, pencils and paper;
- audio or video tape recorders;
- dictaphone.

Gathering the information

Individual children take an adult on a tour of the outdoor space. They can be given control of the route of the tour and how their preferences are recorded during the tour, and how they will be documented later.

   Ask open questions, such as 'what happens now in this part of the garden?'

Making sense of the information

Invite children to share their thoughts with other children or staff. Looking at the photographs, drawings or recordings will promote further discussion about the newly developed space and ensure that staff draw an accurate conclusion about children's views.

Issues to consider

Keep an open mind and try not to make assumptions about the information children provide. For example, for some children the importance of particular areas of the garden is strongly linked to whether or not it is associated with social interaction with friends rather than to the new equipment or features that are sited there. Also, an initial evaluation of children's views about their new space is likely to be influenced by the very newness of the space or feature, i.e. some children may be particularly drawn to it because of the novelty, while others may actively avoid it until they feel more accustomed to it.

Involving children in 'Evaluating and enjoying'

Surveying the space: tours with an intermediary, such as a puppet or soft toy

When to use this activity

Useful technique for:

- identifying the impact of changes and new features;
- gathering children's perspectives on the new developments;
- reviewing the space before and after any developments (see 'Getting started', Prompt sheet 2.3);
- identifying future priorities;
- identifying emerging favourite and important places;
- children under three years old;
- children with limited or undeveloped communication skills.

Use this activity to build up detailed information about what children feel about their newly developed outdoor space. The use of an intermediary, such as a named puppet or soft toy, can provide a focus for the survey with very young children. It is also a useful technique if the adult conducting the survey is not well known to the children; they may be reluctant to share their thoughts with an unfamiliar adult but will be happy to talk to the toy. Alternatively, very young children with a limited vocabulary or those with communication difficulties can use the soft toy to show an adult what they like or dislike in different parts of the garden (see Clark and Moss 2005: 102).

Preparation and resources

Introduce the puppet or toy, or use one that is already known to the children. It is easier if the puppet has a name for children and adults to refer to it by, for example 'Bertie'.

Consider taking photographs as a record of the tour findings and to act as a catalyst for further discussions among staff and children.

Offer children some options for recording their thoughts, for example through drawings, photographs or tape recordings.

Gathering the information

Individual children take 'Bertie' and an adult on a tour of the outdoor space. Either allow children to choose the route of the tour or ask them to show 'Bertie' where particular experiences take place.

Ask open questions, such as 'Can you show/tell Bertie what happens now in this part of the garden?' or 'If Bertie wanted to hide in the garden where would he go?'

Making sense of the information

Invite the children involved in the tour to share their thoughts with other children or staff. To promote further discussion about the space create a book using photographs or children's drawings. Create a display using 'Bertie' and captioned photographs that identify what children think he could do in each part of the garden.

Issues to consider

Keep an open mind; children's perspectives on the best place for 'Bertie' to go for particular experiences may differ from the adult view and from the original plans for the space.

The use of an intermediary can enable children to open up about more sensitive issues, such as why they have strong preferences for, or an aversion to, particular parts of the garden. These insights will need careful consideration by everyone involved in reviewing the achievements of the project and identifying priorities for any further developments.

Involving children in 'Evaluating and enjoying'

Finding out how children feel about the newly developed outdoor environment: happy tokens

When to use this activity

Useful technique for:

- active children who like to be on the move;
- identifying children's preferences in the new environment;
- gathering opinions about new features in the environment;
- identifying new features, items or activities of emerging importance to the child;
- reviewing how children feel about the space before and after any developments (see 'Getting started', Prompt sheet 2.5).

Preparation and resources

Gather together several containers and some tokens. The tokens can be anything that is in plentiful supply, for example bricks, beads or buttons. However, take care that the size of the token does not represent a choking hazard to very young children.

Label the containers with a happy or sad face and a note of where they are to be sited. Place them in pairs around the outdoor area in key spots, for example by new features or changed spaces.

Gathering the information

Encourage children who visit each area to collect a token and drop it into the pot with the face that represents how they feel about the new feature or changed space.

Making sense of the information

By counting the number of tokens in each pot it will be easy to establish emerging preferences for particular areas of the garden. This may confirm the success of the original plans or may provide indicators of unforeseen problems. Children can help to count and collate the information onto a summary sheet.

Issues to consider

Some children may not have a strong preference for a particular area. Therefore it may be appropriate to introduce a third pot labelled with a neutral expression to allow these children to express their viewpoint.

It is possible to determine preferences linked to gender or age by giving children preordained tokens; for example, by using a particular colour or shape of token for boys/girls, or for children under/over three years old. This will provide useful additional details that can be used to inform any further developments.

Involving children in 'Evaluating and enjoying'

Finding out how children feel about the improvements to their outdoor environment: cheer rating

When to use this activity

Useful technique for:

- active children who like to be on the move;
- identifying children's preferences in the newly developed environment;
- reviewing the space before and after any developments (see 'Getting started', Prompt sheet 2.6).

Preparation and resources

This activity needs little preparation or resources. It is a very useful evaluative activity that can be used to get children familiar with the process of giving an opinion on aspects of their new outdoor environment. Children express their preferences and levels of enthusiasm for different parts of the garden by cheering in each area. A tape recorder is a useful way to record children's responses.

Gathering the information

Having explained the activity to the children, visit each part of the garden with a small group and encourage them to cheer – loudly or quietly according to how they feel about the space. Consider using a tape recorder to document children's responses. Remember to mention on tape where each cheer takes place to help make sense of the recording afterwards.

Making sense of the information

It will be possible to form a general view about how children feel about the developments, based on their cheer responses. This may confirm the view of adults in the setting or may offer new perspectives.

Issues to consider

This activity does not reveal accurate measurable information; however, it is fun and it will provide a broad overview about how children feel.

6 The legacy of the Space to Grow project

What is happening now?

Between 2003 and 2005 each setting worked through a cyclical process of change, to audit their existing practice, identify areas of development, make changes and improvements, and then begin the process again by re-auditing their practice. Almost ten years later, in 2012, the project settings were invited to give an update for this second edition of *Creating A Space to Grow*. Of the twenty-two settings originally involved, four are no longer registered as childcare providers. The remaining eighteen settings were contacted and of those eight responded. These eight settings were invited to provide an update on their current use of outdoors to identify whether the changes they made had been sustainable over time, and whether they had continued to improve their practice and meet the original aims of the project. The legacy of the Space to Grow project is the positive impact it continues to have on the settings involved. A member of staff at St Martin's Preschool in Dover echoed the views of many practitioners when she summed up the outcomes of the project 'it was the catalyst for everything we have done since'. The following case studies provide a snapshot of the current outdoor provision at the eight settings that were revisited.

Case study 6.1 Bertie's Nursery, Faversham

In 2010, Bertie's Nursery moved to new premises at Davington Primary School. Despite having had to leave behind the garden they created as part of the Space to Grow project, the staff and children have settled happily into the building and are now developing their new outdoor space. The building has a well-equipped transition area where staff and children can prepare for going outdoors. Everyone is provided with waterproofs to ensure they are able to enjoy going outdoors whatever the weather! The emphasis the leadership and management place on using outdoors effectively is evident through policies, newsletters, job descriptions and recruitment processes. It is a clear expectation that staff and volunteers will spend time outdoors. Plans for children's learning and next steps are built around their current interests and always include possible outdoor experiences. Good use is also made of spontaneous events, such as the sudden fall of autumn leaves in the garden,

which provided a morning of child-initiated leaf play. Storage sheds are well organised with boxes of labelled equipment that are easily accessible to develop play and support learning, and staff are quick to respond to children's ideas and offer further equipment or materials to enrich their play.

A visit from Ofsted soon after the nursery relocated judged the overall provision as outstanding and included the following comments about the outdoor provision:

> Children are enthusiastic, inquisitive learners who are eager to attend the nursery and explore the excellent opportunities offered to them. They are confident individuals who develop their independent skills, making choices throughout the nursery, both indoors and outdoors...Children use an excellent range of resources to learn about the world around them. They use sticks from the large trees in the garden and enjoy exploring the properties of mud with their wellington boots and hands. They have opportunities to explore sand and water, from filling and emptying containers, to painting with water outside. A wide variety of additional resources in storage boxes enables children to use their senses, feeling wood, pebbles and sea shells...Children have constant opportunities to engage in a wide range of physical activities, both indoors and outdoors to gain a secure understanding about the importance of regular exercise and fresh air. Children display well-developed independent skills putting on their coats and wellingtons to play outside, supporting their healthy lifestyle.

Ditton Church Preschool, Ditton

The garden at Ditton Church Preschool is a thriving and well used outdoor space. Many of the original features created during the project are still in use, however, the shingle pit has been built over by the Church and some surfaces have been changed. At the time this reduced the space slightly, however, five years ago an additional plot of land next door was made available by the Church to the preschool and consequently the outdoor space has doubled in size overall. In 2011 the setting's Ofsted report judged that:

> The setting's outdoor play area, however is the most prominent element, and children have access to an exceptionally rich and stimulating outdoor area; with a highly diverse and well prepared range of play and learning opportunities. Children have a range of play houses, a large messy play area, and children enjoy a lot of tactile and sensory learning; as well using a large grass area for games and physical play.

In recognition of the importance of the outdoor environment, a member of the management committee and one of the staff have been allocated specific responsibility for co-ordinating the use and maintenance of the garden. Consequently the outdoor environment is promoted in many aspects of the preschool practice, including through recruitment processes, photographs and displays, children's records and in discussions with parents. The outdoor space is also regularly reviewed to develop it further and to ensure it meets the needs of the children attending. The physical environment has several blind spots meaning that children may not always be within sight of staff. Staff are aware that it is a requirement of the EYFS that children are usually within sight and always within hearing and they have taken a positive approach to complying with this requirement; the garden is risk assessed to ensure that any hazards are minimised, and the staff:child ratios are kept high, ensuring that there is always someone available to keep an eye on the less visible parts of the garden. The preschool provides all-weather protection for children and ask that parents supply wellies when necessary. Staff have taken a deliberate decision to encourage children to manage their own clothing with only minimal help. This is working well, children quickly become independent since they are motivated to learn how to put on their wellies and coats by their desire to get outdoors. Everyone is less frustrated, and staff are able to spend more time supporting children's play rather than sorting out coats!

Case study 6.3 **Glebe House Day Nursery, Larkfield**

Glebe House Day Nursery has expanded their outdoor environment and increased the number of areas that children can access. Children in the baby room continue to have free-flow access to the small balcony area and staff value the extra space and experiences it provides for babies. Babies also use a more recently created outdoor space at the rear of the nursery. The owner reports that emphasis placed on outdoors is embedded in recruitment processes, tours for new parents and curriculum delivery. Much of the garden has been surfaced to increase year-round use, however, in recognition of the importance of unstructured play in natural environments, one part of the garden has deliberately been left in an undeveloped state. Staff report that children love going into this space to dig, make mud pies, and discover mini-beasts. To facilitate their independent access to this area a transition space has been created where wellies are kept in readiness for the next muddy adventure.

Case study 6.4 **Happy Faces Preschool, Tonbridge**

Happy Faces Preschool has gone from strength to strength and now has an extension to the original building. Although this has reduced the size of the outdoor space, the setting continues to value the outdoor environment and staff ensure that children have opportunities to go outside throughout the session. A large covered area now provides shelter and protection from extreme weather conditions. A new climbing structure has replaced some of the original features that were created as part of the project and the planting that has grown up over the years has softened the impact of the anti-vandal fencing that was once so prominent. The setting's leadership and the staff team recognise that outdoor play has a positive impact on children's health and well-being and it is promoted through policies, newsletters, displays, planning documents and children's records. The leadership team also spend time outdoors themselves; this allows them to model good practice and support staff and volunteers who are less confident about being outdoors.

Case study 6.5 **Highways at Hamstreet Kindergarten, Hamstreet**

The outdoor environment at Highways at Hamstreet Kindergarten has undergone significant changes in recent years. Having secured funding for a much needed new building, the upheaval of the building programme meant that the features and structures in the garden had to be dismantled and rebuilt. The preschool held two 'Garden Days' and staff and parents worked hard to reinstate everything in the garden once the builders had left. The preschool now has free-flow access into the reinstated garden through wide glass doors.

Staff continue to prioritise outdoor play and have embraced the Forest School approach to using outdoors. A member of the staff team is a trained Forest School Leader and the children have regular access to woods next to the school. In 2009 Ofsted judged that:

> All children make outstanding progress in their learning and development because of a well-planned curriculum that provides an inclusive and stimulating environment both indoors and outdoors. The award winning outside area is used in all weathers, to maximum effect to develop children's learning. It is a stimulating, captivating environment, designed to encourage hands-on learning, creative play and problem solving. Here, children get absorbed in myriad activities, for example, having a tea party in the 'twigwam', being enthralled by the tadpoles in the 'pond' or exploring and devising construction tasks in the digging area. There is a good balance of adult and child led activities. For example, one adult-led activity was 'metal detecting' using numbered frogs with paper clips attached.

The leadership and management at Highways at Hamstreet Kindergarten continue to place significant value on outdoor learning. As Figure 6.1 shows, this ethos has impacted on all aspects of their provision and practice.

Children have sufficient space to be with others or to be alone	There are quiet areas with benches and logs where children can sit if they want to be alone. There are also plenty of opportunities for them to be with others as they play in the mud digging area, large sand pit and twigwam.
Children have challenging opportunities to be physically active	We are lucky to have a large garden with different areas which enable the children to be physically active Activities include mud digging, sand play, climbing and jumping from tyres, monkey bars and a range of bikes and scooters.
The outdoor space has secure boundaries	There is fencing all around the garden. There is one locked gate which parents use when the main school gates are closed and a smaller wooden gate which leads into the playground.
The environment changes and evolves as children's play develops	Children use different materials and equipment in the garden to develop their ideas and make changes. They build with materials such as logs, bricks and planks and use equipment such as blankets, tents and sheets to build in the garden.
The space has a variety of levels and surfaces	We have grass, decking, bark chipping, mud and sand and a tarmac path. Also tree stumps, wooden logs and sloping areas in the garden.
There are places for shade and shelter	There are trees, a slide which they can shelter under, a twig-wam and tents. Next steps...it would be nice to be able to shelter from the rain during a very heavy downpour without having to go inside.
Children and adults have all-weather protection and there is spare clothing	We have plenty of outdoor suits; enough for wet outdoor play in the morning and afternoon every day. The staff also have waterproof coats and trousers to wear so they can interact fully with the children. All children bring in wellies and store them at nursery.
All children have independent access to outdoors	We have free flow play in the morning and in the afternoon where children can choose to play indoors or outside if they prefer.
There are safe places to sit and watch the world go by	There are lots of places for children to sit, for example in the twigwam, on the seats around the oak tree or on the bench by the nursery doors. Next steps...there are not many places for the adults to sit whilst interacting with the children.
The environment is full of irresistible open-ended play materials	We have real bricks, planks and logs. We have large and small branches and sticks. We also have nets, cushions, materials, pegs, chairs and tents.
Equipment is well organised and there are child-friendly accessible storage facilities	We have dustbins for sand, water and digging resources. We also have a sheltered area the children are able to access where the bikes and cars are kept.

Figure 6.1 Highways at Hamstreet Kindergarten – self audit of practice and provision

Children have access to water for play and gardening	There are two taps in the garden which the children can access. Watering cans and buckets are kept outside in dustbins and are freely available to children.
On a daily basis children have extended time to play outdoors...	We have free flow play every morning and afternoon and we also work outside during adult directed group work – either in the garden or in the woodland next to the school.
Practitioners are attentive and engaged outdoors – they play alongside children and sensitively introduce new ideas, language and skills	Practitioners all wear waterproof clothing and wellies so even in bad weather they are able to get down to the child's level and explore areas of the garden with them and scaffold their learning.
Practitioners are confident, knowledgeable, playful and enthusiastic about being outdoors...	Practitioners are always excited about being outside in all weathers. We encourage the children to participate in many outdoor activities and always ensure that they are wearing protective clothing.
Practitioners create an environment that values children's interests, and they plan further experiences that build on children's play ideas	The outdoor environment has been carefully planned to allow the children lots of opportunities to explore and follow their interests which we then help to encourage and hopefully develop further.
Daily routines enable the effective use of outdoors ● Free-flow access and flexible deployment enables staff and children to move freely between indoors and outdoors. ● Children's opportunities to be outdoors are not overly restricted by care routines (e.g. snacks and meals, rest and sleep, toileting and nappy changes) ● The set up/tidy up routines outdoors are minimal and involve both staff and the children.	During our free flow time we have staff inside and outside so that the children can come and go as they please. Our snack bar is open during free flow play so the children can access it if they want to. Children help to put out equipment and materials like paint and chalks etc. They are encouraged to help tidy away the bikes and the sand area and to collect things that need to be put away indoors.
Practitioners consider and include use of the outdoor environment when planning next steps for children's learning and development	We use the garden as an extension of the classroom and most activities that we plan can be implimented indoors or outside.

Figure 6.1 continued

The setting leadership and management team promote the value placed on outdoors. E.g. through: • publicity and marketing materials • job descriptions • policies • development plans • budgets • staff training days prospectus and other information for parents	We invite parents to donate equipment and materials for the garden such as plant, flowers, cooking equipment etc. and to help us maintain it on Garden days held throughout the year. In job descriptions we always ask for employees to have a 'love of learning outdoors'. We have a garden policy which describes and sets out our aims and objectives when using the garden. We always tell prospective parents about our garden and explain its role in our curriculum.

Figure 6.1 continued

Case study 6.6 Little Acorns Preschool, Herne

At Little Acorns Preschool the staff and management committee have embraced outdoor learning and as the accompanying images show, the outdoor space has been transformed! The boundary fencing has been re-sited to provide a larger play area, and new structures have been created including a large well-organised shelter that acts as a transition zone between indoors and outdoors and gives children independent access to resources they may need to support their play.

In 2009 Ofsted made the following judgements and comments about the use of outdoors:

Overall the quality of the provision is outstanding… children enjoy a very wide range of exciting and imaginative activities and make first rate progress. Children are active learners. A free flow of activities from inside to outside ensures that children have freedom to learn and play in the spacious and very well equipped learning areas. Children delight in running after the assistants in the garden who pretend to be flying dinosaurs… Children can watch the birds from an observation platform taking food from feeders. Skilled assistants talk to the children about what they are doing and what they can see. Children's vocabulary and knowledge are developing well.

The value placed on outdoors is embedded in the ethos and working practices, such as the recruitment and training of staff, the employment of a

In 2005 the development of the garden was beginning

In 2013 it is established and thriving

In 2003

In 2013

handyman to maintain the equipment and the development of a staff garden so practitioners can enjoy being outdoors during their breaks. The setting has also adopted the Forest School approach to outdoor learning. Two members of staff are Forest School Leaders and the setting has recently acquired the lease of local woodland. The intention is that all children starting at the preschool have six Forest School sessions and then, once they are confident and comfortable in the woodland environment, they will have the opportunity to visit it on a daily basis for natural play sessions.

Case study 6.7 Saplings@The Sports Centre, Tunbridge Wells

The staff at Saplings@The Sports Centre have continued to work hard to develop their outdoor space. Although they are based upstairs without easy access, practitioners have created a familiar routine that everyone follows to get down the stairs and outside. The garden now has a sensory area and raised beds for vegetables. Planting along the boundary fencing has been established and this provides some screening between the setting and the adjacent secondary school. The access hatch is still in use by students wishing to reclaim lost footballs. The shed installed as part of the original project has stood the test of time and is now a well-organised 'outdoor classroom'. Posters and factual books about outdoors make it an attractive space, and low-level shelving ensures children have independent access to additional outdoor play materials. In 2009 Ofsted judged that:

> Staff recognise the importance of outdoor play. Whilst the location of the group room does not make it possible for children to flow freely into the outdoor play area, they are taken outside every day that weather permits. They engage in physical play as well as investigating and enjoying nature.

The nursery is part of a small chain of local nurseries and the senior management provides a clear message through the termly newsletter to ensure that the value of outdoor learning is understood by parents (see Figure 6.2). The garden is still evolving; children are currently making their own stepping stones from recycled materials, and parents are involved in 'garden days' to maintain the momentum, and to share the value of outdoor learning.

Longacre Link

www.longacrechildcare.co.uk

Issue: 011 Date: Summer 2012

Parental Circular for nurseries managed by Longacre Childcare Ltd

Across our three nurseries we offer a combination of care and education that encompasses not only requirements of the Early Years Foundation Stage and the importance of outdoor play but also the teaching methods of Maria Montessori.

Outdoor Learning

Enjoyment of the outdoors

Using open space to fulfill basic childhood needs – jumping, running, climbing, swinging, racing, yelling, rolling, hiding, and making a big mess is what childhood is all about! For a variety of obvious reasons many of these things cannot occur indoors. Children need to have these important experiences. Our Outdoor Environments are designed to fulfill children's basic needs for freedom, adventure, experimentation, risk-taking, and just being children

Learning about the world

Outdoor play enables young children to learn lots and lots and lots of things about the world. How does ice feel and sound? Can sticks stand up in sand? How do plants grow? How does mud feel? How does the overhang of the building create cool shade from the sun? What does a chrysalis change into?

In the outside environment at the Longacre Nurseries the children learn maths, science, ecology, gardening, ornithology, construction, farming, vocabulary, the seasons, the various times of the day, and all about the local weather. Not only do children learn lots of basic and fundamental information about how the world works in a very effective manner, they are more likely to remember what they learned because it was concrete and personally meaningful.

Learning about self and the environment

We encourage children to learn about their own physical and emotional capabilities. In order to do this children must push their limits. How high can I swing? Do I dare go down the slide? How high can I climb? Can I go down the slide headfirst? In order to learn about the physical world, the child needs to experiment with the physical world by asking questions: Can I slide on the sand? Can I roll on grass? What happens when I throw a piece of wood into the pond?

An essential task of development is appreciating how we fit into the natural order of things – animals, plants, the weather, and so on.

Health

We believe outdoor play enables children to enjoy the natural environment and learn to seek out exercise, fresh air, and activity. There is something fundamentally healthy about using the outdoors. Outdoor play develops physical activity, and an understanding of how to care for the environment. Children who learn to enjoy the outdoors are much more likely to become adults who enjoy outdoor activities.

How to Encourage Different Kinds of Play

We divide outdoor play into the following areas and activities:

Physical play: In general, physical play should be encouraged by climbing equipment and swings, tricycle paths, and large areas of grass and hills on which pre-schoolers can run and crawl and infants and toddlers can lie, crawl, and roll. Tricycle paths are used for Big Toys,

tricycles, scooters, balls, jogging, and wagons. Climbing equipment for infants and toddlers should be very basic.

Constructive play: Research continually shows that constructive play is the pre-schooler's favourite kind of play, probably because they can and do control it. Constructive play is encouraged by using sand and water play, providing a place for art, woodwork and blocks, wheeled toys, and lots of loose objects throughout the outdoor area.

Social play: Children need lots of opportunities outside to develop basic social skills and social competencies: pushing each other on the swing, pulling a wagon carrying another child, playing together in the sand, and so on. Projects such as gardening, observing the weather, and having a picnic can be – social activities.

Longacre Childcare Ltd • 01732 462339 • longacrechildcare@tiscali.co.uk • www.longacrechildcare.co.uk

Figure 6.2

How we achieve all this at Longacre Childcare

The Longacre childcare staff members really do make the most of the wonderful garden areas and outdoor classrooms they have at their disposal. The staff always give the best care possible to the children in all aspects of their day at the Nursery, from morning snack to afternoon tea to going home and everything that happens in between.

The children at Longacre Day Nursery have also been enjoying their garden area. The children and their teddies were all treated to a Teddy Bear's Picnic. They have been learning how to play croquet and they have enjoyed building dens using lots of different bits and pieces they found around the nursery and in the garden. Lots of different ball games have been played and they have even had time for a Mini Beast Hunt and for growing different seeds and flowers

The children at Saplings were certainly not going to be left out of the garden fun. They enjoyed holding a Jubilee Garden Party complete with a visit from The Queen herself! The threat of some rather large grey clouds could not even dampen the children's excitement!

The children at Broughton Cottage Day Nursery have been able to watch the newly sewn grass seeds grow during the last few months.

They have enjoyed their football coaching lessons in the outdoor area and they have even managed to have their afternoon tea in the garden on a few occasions, despite the challenges posed by the weather!

They have also enjoyed nature trails, playing with bubbles, digging for mini beasts and they have also been busy planting vegetables and plants. They have even found time to help Bev (their Montessori Teacher) in the Herb Garden.

Staying Safe in the Sun

The sun is an important part of our lives. Sunny days have a positive impact on our mood, increase our level of physical activity, make many social events and gatherings possible, and even benefit our health by providing our bodies with essential vitamin D. Unfortunately, sun exposure also presents risk factors that can lead to serious health issues. It's important to learn what you can do to protect yourself and how to spot any possible signs of skin cancer.

Sun Safety for Children

At Longacre Childcare we adhere to the following guidelines:

Babies under 6 months old should never be exposed to the sun. Cover their skin and feet protectively. To protect their head and face, choose a wide-brimmed hat or bonnet, and use a pushchair with a canopy or hood.

Children- need to be active. Activities like playing outdoors are vital to their physical health. Always apply sunscreen as part of your child's "getting ready to play" rituals. Encourage shade-friendly activities during peak sun hours.

Here are some easy ways to protect you and your children from the Sun

1. **Wear sunscreen with a SPF 15 or higher.** If you or your children have fair skin or light hair, you are more susceptible to the sun's rays

2. **Use waterproof sunscreen** to make sure it stays on longer, even if you perspire or get wet.

3. **Reapply sunscreen often** – usually every two hours, but sooner if you've been swimming or are perspiring heavily.

4. **Seek shade or avoid the sun during the peak hours of 10am – 4pm.** The sun is strongest during those hours, even on cloudy days.

5. **Wear a hat** Encourage your children to wear hats to help shade their eyes, ears and head.

6. **Wear lightweight, loose-fitting clothing that protects a larger area of your skin** such as long-sleeve shirts or long trousers.

Remember To Drink Plenty of Water and Stay Sun Safe.

Have a wonderful Summer!

Longacre Childcare Ltd • 01732 462339 • longacrechildcare@tiscali.co.uk • www.longacrechildcare.co.uk

Figure 6.2 continued

In 2005 St Martin's Preschool was under threat of closure with a partially condemned building and low numbers. However, now under different leadership, it is a thriving setting with a rosy future. In 2010 the preschool's Ofsted report reported that:

> Children really enjoy the freedom to choose if they play inside or in the garden, and given the choice they choose to play outside. This free-flow system works very well in practice and allows children full independence. Staff have ambitious ideas to transform the garden into a fully operational outdoor learning area and plans are well established. They have started a vegetable patch so that children can learn about growing, harvesting and eating the produce. There are further plans to make the outside environment sustainable by taking the current recycling further to include composting and water collection.

The outdoor area has already been extended and now includes a playhouse, a willow tunnel, sandpit, pergola, raised gardening beds and an all-weather surface. Further developments are planned, including a sheltered transition zone. The commitment to outdoor play is embedded in daily working practices and staff are described as 'motivated and enthusiastic' about going outdoors. The emphasis placed on outdoors is highlighted to prospective parents in the prospectus. Children have free-flow access to the garden throughout the session and the staff follow children's interests and support their play. All staff and children have waterproofs and wellies provided by the preschool in order that outdoor play can continue whatever the weather!

Improving your outdoor practice

It is clear from the settings involved in the Space to Grow project that good outdoor practice has several key elements and involves much more than a shed of resources! Some project settings had one specific challenge, such as improving access, whilst other settings had a combination of challenges, such as gaining parental support, improving practitioner knowledge and reorganising storage. *Outdoor Matters!* believes that the common challenges faced by practitioners fall into one of three categories; workforce, environment and practice (see Figure 6.3).

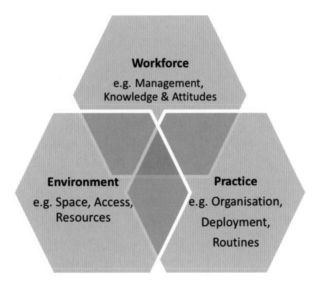

Figure 6.3 A diagram illustrating the interrelated and holistic nature of the key elements of good outdoor practice; workforce, practice, environment.

© Outdoor Matters

These three elements are interrelated and of equal importance. When combined they are an effective framework for enhancing outdoor provision and practices in early years settings. Improvements to the use of outdoors require action from everyone in the setting across all three elements.

The following checklist identifies specific 'indicators of good outdoor practice' within these three elements, and supports self-evaluation of current outdoor practice. A photocopiable version of this checklist is at the end of this chapter.

Workforce

Leaders and managers promote and demonstrate the value placed on outdoors through:

- modelling good practice and being outdoors themselves in all weathers;
- publicity and marketing materials;
- job descriptions and recruitment processes;
- policies;
- development plans;
- budgets;
- staff training days;
- prospectus, notice boards, displays and other information for parents.

Practitioners are confident, knowledgeable, playful and enthusiastic about being outdoors.

- Valuing the outdoor environment and understanding the benefits for children.
- Demonstrating a positive attitude towards being outdoors.
- Dressing appropriately for the weather conditions.
- Supporting risk-taking and undertaking risk assessments to enable children's experiences rather than restrict them.
- Considering and including use of the outdoor environment when planning next steps for children's learning and development.
- Being attentive and engaged outdoors – playing alongside children and sensitively introducing new ideas, language and skills.

Environment

Practitioners create an enabling outdoor environment that:

- values children's interests, and supports the development of further experiences that build on children's play ideas;
- provides children with sufficient space to be with others or to be alone;
- offers children challenging opportunities to be physically active;
- has secure boundaries;
- changes and evolves as children's play develops;
- has a variety of levels and surfaces;
- has places for shade and shelter;
- has safe places to sit and watch the world go by;
- is full of irresistible open-ended play materials;
- Gives children access to water for play and gardening.

Practice

The setting's organisation, deployment of staff and daily routines take account of the value of outdoors and ensure that:

- children have extended time to play outdoors on a daily basis;
- children and adults have all-weather protection, and there is spare clothing;
- all children have independent access to outdoors;
- equipment is well organised;
- there are child-friendly accessible storage facilities;
- free-flow access and flexible deployment enables staff and children to move freely between indoors and outdoors;
- Children's opportunities to be outdoors are not overly restricted by care routines (e.g. snacks and meals, rest and sleep, toileting and nappy changes) or by timetabled school activities, such as PE, assembly or breaktime.

Managing change to improve practice: The *Outdoor Matters!* approach

The Space to Grow settings have proved that positive change is possible and sustainable, and they have also shown that developments outdoors require time, energy, enthusiasm and commitment from everyone at the setting. I suggest using a cyclical approach to managing change and improving practice to ensure that the improvements are successful and sustainable in the longer term (see Figure 6.4). The summary of this process is set out below and first appeared as an article featured in the management supplement of *Nursery World* magazine in September 2012.

'*Managing Change to Improve Practice*'

Figure 6.4 The cyclical approach to managing change used by *Outdoor Matters!*

Review

Before making any changes it is important to evaluate existing practice. Using the bulleted lists above, start to review your current practice under the three headings: workforce, environment and practice. Aim to agree what is working well and also to identify the areas for improvement. To gather a truly representative viewpoint involve as many people as you can in this audit, including children, parents and practitioners along with non-teaching staff such as caretakers, cleaners, office staff and midday supervisors. Remember that there will be a range of valid perspectives within the team. For example, the cleaner may feel that the muddy footprints to the cloakroom are a negative aspect of the current use of outdoors, whilst the practitioners may see muddy trails as an inevitable consequence of successful free-flow. Consider all the possible sources of evidence that could inform your decisions, for example:

- discussion with children, parents and colleagues;
- observation of outdoor area in use;
- review of planning;
- review of children's records;
- review of displays and notice boards;
- scrutiny of information, policies and paperwork;
- review of resources and equipment storage.

Plan

Once you have clear evaluation of the aspects that are working well, and those that need development, you can start to plan your next steps. Think about who to involve in action planning; it is good practice to share the responsibility for planning improvements across the staff team and to also involve parents, children and non-teaching staff. This ensures that the planned changes are agreed and understood by all and makes maintaining the improvements in the longer term a more likely outcome. Many settings have had success in creating a working group that meets regularly to focus on the development process. Begin by working out whether you have identified the need for improvements across all three elements or just one or two. If there is a lot to do you will need to prioritise and set realistic timescales. Try and work out whether there is an underlying concern that is limiting children's outdoor experiences, such as staff knowledge and confidence? It is important to tackle these core issues as a priority, but try and also identify some 'quick wins' – changes that are easy and quick to accomplish at regular intervals, and make everyone feel as though things are actually happening. 'Quick wins' such as sorting out the shed, creating a display of outdoor learning or putting together a box of den-building resources will help to maintain morale and a sense of momentum whilst the bigger issues get sorted more slowly. An action plan is a working document, it should not be created and then filed! It will need regular reviewing and amending as some actions are completed and further tasks are identified. Use it to record your actions, as well as timescales, responsibilities, funding requirements and measures for indicating you have been successful.

Do

The next stage in the process is the implementation of your action plan. In this instance it is important to use people's skills and enthusiasms within the working party and across the whole setting. For example, one parent may be able to take on responsibility for fundraising and grant applications, whilst someone else may prefer to trawl boot fairs for wellies. Be realistic in your timescales and expect some setbacks. For example, if a setting decides to offer snacks outdoors as well as indoors at first it is likely that all children will choose to have their snack outdoors the moment it is made available – and the ensuing chaos may cause practitioners to say 'we tried it and it didn't work'. It is usually worth persevering, since once children get used to being able to choose where and when to have a snack they will relax and choose whatever suits them on a given day. If staff initially feel overwhelmed, remind them that new ways of doing things take time to become embedded, so it is to be expected that the early days of a new routine or significant change will feel chaotic as everyone adjusts. Suggest that any new initiatives are trialled for six weeks, then have a formal review at the end of this period to identify what worked and what needs tweaking. This review session by all those involved is a useful strategy to mark the end of one full cycle of the change process, and identify what needs to happen in the next cycle to continue the improvement of the outdoor space.

Who can help?

The Kent Space to Grow project was an innovative approach to improving outdoor practice. Developed and delivered by Learning through Landscapes, and funded by the Kent Early Years and Childcare Partnership, the combination of sustained support, a funding award and ongoing access to advice and information has proved to be a successful way of creating sustainable changes and improvements to outdoor practice.

Ten years on, awareness of the importance of outdoors is much higher amongst early years practitioners, however, many settings still face challenges similar to those that were tackled in

Kent. Whatever the problems are, whether it is a lack of confidence amongst staff, poor access, disorganised resources, anxieties amongst parents or difficulties managing mud, most challenges can be overcome. Although lots of practitioners will have the confidence to work through the process of change outlined in this book without external help, some settings value an external opinion to help the review process, the identification of next steps, and the creation of an Outdoor Improvement Plan. Learning through Landscapes and *Outdoor Matters!* both provide information, support and advice settings and schools across the UK.

Outdoor Matters!

I believe that all young children deserve high quality outdoor curriculum experiences delivered in this unique and special environment by knowledgeable, enthusiastic and playful practitioners. *Outdoor Matters!* is the consultancy service I offer to schools and settings, early years providers and organisations wanting to improve their outdoor practice. Drawing on thirty years of professional knowledge, a practical and creative approach to overcoming problems and a genuine understanding of the challenges practitioners face, I provide information and support to the early years sector through advisory visits, training, conferences, projects and the *Outdoor Matters!* website; www.outdoormatters.co.uk.

Learning through Landscapes

Learning through Landscapes is the UK charity dedicated to enhancing outdoor learning and play for children. Their vision is that every child benefits from stimulating outdoor learning and play in their education. They aim to enable children to connect with nature, be more active, be more engaged with their learning, develop their social skills and have fun! They do this through three avenues by advocating the benefits of outdoor learning and play, inspiring and enabling the design and development of outdoor environments to support children's development, and inspiring and enabling teachers and early years practitioners to develop the confidence, ideas and skills they need to make better use of outdoor spaces.

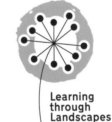

Learning through Landscapes

Learning through Landscapes is the only UK charity specialising in outdoor learning and play in education. Their knowledge and expertise is based on more than twenty years' experience of practical action and research. www.ltl.org.uk

Self reflection tool for skilled and thoughtful practitioners

How effectively do I support children's outdoor learning?

EYFS Theme	Characteristic/skill	Rating 0–5 comments
A Unique Child	Showing <u>genuine</u> interest in the children's ideas and play	
	Celebrating with children their interests and achievements	
	Valuing and acting upon children's suggestions (even when they are not in line with what we had expected/planned)	
Positive Relationships	Establishing a strong bond with EVERY child in my key person group	
	Supporting children to resolve their own conflicts (rather than solving them for them)	
	Encouraging and supporting children to persevere through difficulties and to take risks	
	Being sensitive to each child's thinking and learning	
	Respecting and allowing time for thinking/contemplation	
Enabling Environments	Ensuring children have sustained time to develop child-initiated activities	
	Facilitating children's free (and free-flow) use of rich outdoor spaces	
	Joining in play and child-initiated activity following children's agendas	
	Frequently replenishing and varying resources, using fresh and surprising approaches	
	Scaffolding children's learning through talk, discussing strategies and ideas, suggesting possibilities and modelling approaches	
Learning and Development	Providing first-hand experiences to explore and discover	
	Directly teaching, through demonstrating or explaining	
	Using the language of learning to focus children on themselves as learners	
	Being knowledgeable about child development. Identifying and supporting next steps in outdoor learning	

Adapted from Learning, Playing and Interacting Good Practice in the Early Years Foundation Stage 00775-2009BKT-EN p27

Evaluating and improving your outdoor practice

Good outdoor practice has several elements and involves much more than a shed of resources! This diagram illustrates the interrelated and holistic nature of the key elements of good practice; workforce, practice, environment. Each aspect is of equal importance in securing high quality outdoor provision and practices in early years settings.

Outdoor Matters has developed a checklist that identifies indicators of good outdoor practice. Use this checklist to evaluate your current outdoor practice and identify your priorities for development. Remember, improvements to the use of outdoors takes time and require commitment and action from everyone in the setting.

Rate your existing practice 1-5 where 1 = priority for development and 5 = this is a strength

	1	2	3	4	5

Workforce:

Leaders and Managers promote and demonstrate the value placed on outdoors through:
- modelling good practice and being outdoors themselves in all weathers
- publicity and marketing materials
- job descriptions and recruitment processes
- policies
- budgets and development plans
- staff training days
- prospectus, notice boards, displays and other information for parents

Practitioners are confident, knowledgeable, playful and enthusiastic about being outdoors
- Valuing the outdoor environment and understand the benefits for children
- Demonstrating a positive attitude towards being outdoors
- Dressing appropriately for the weather conditions
- Supporting risk taking and risk assess to enable children's experiences rather than restrict them
- Considering and including use of the outdoor environment when planning next steps for children's learning and development
- Being attentive and engaged outdoors – playing alongside children and sensitively introducing new ideas, language and skills

	Rate your existing practice 1–5 where 1 = priority for development and 5 = this is a strength				
	1	2	3	4	5
Environment: Practitioners create an enabling outdoor environment that • Values children's interests, and supports the development of further experiences that build on children's play ideas • Provides children with sufficient space to be with others or to be alone • Offers children challenging opportunities to be physically active • Has secure boundaries • Changes and evolves as children's play develops • Has a variety of levels and surfaces • Has places for shade and shelter • Has safe places to sit and watch the world go by • Is full of irresistible open-ended play materials • Gives children access to water for play and gardening					
Practice: The setting's organisation, deployment of staff, and daily routines take account of the value of outdoors and ensure that • Children have extended time to play outdoors on a daily basis • Children and adults have all weather protection, and there is spare clothing • All children have independent access to outdoors • Equipment is well organised • There are child-friendly accessible storage facilities • Free-flow access and flexible deployment enables staff and children to move freely between indoors and outdoors. • Children's opportunities to be outdoors are not overly restricted by care routines (e.g. snacks and meals, rest and sleep, toileting and nappy changes) or by timetabled school activities, such as P.E., Assembly, Breaktime. • The set up/tidy up routines outdoors are minimal, and involve both staff and the children.					

A summary of our priorities:
Look at your scores of 1 and 2 and record three of these priorities next to each heading below – then get Action Planning!

Workforce	
Environment:	
Practice:	

Further reading

Bilton, Helen (2005) *Playing Outisde: Activities, Ideas and Inspiration for the Early Years*. London: David Fulton Publishers.

Clark, Alison (2004) *Why and How We Listen to Young Children*. Listening as a Way of Life series. London: National Children's Bureau.

Clark, Alison and Moss, Peter (2005) *Listening to Young Children: The Mosaic Approach*. London: National Children's Bureau.

Clark, Alison and Moss, Peter (2005) *Spaces to Play: More Listening to Young Children Using the Mosaic Approach*. London: National Children's Bureau.

Dickins, Mary (2004) *Listening to Young Disabled Children*. Listening as a Way of Life series. London: National Children's Bureau.

Dickins, Mary, Emerson, Su and Gordon-Smith, Pat (2004) *Starting with Choice: Inclusive Strategies for Consulting with Young Children*. Save the Children Fund.

Fajerman, Lina and Sutton, Faye (2000) *Children as Partners in Planning*. Save the Children Fund.

Kinney, Linda and McCabe, Jerry (2001) *Children as Partners: a Guide to Consulting with Very Young Children and Empowering them to Participate Effectively*. Stirling Council. (Available from Children's Services, Stirling Council, Viewforth, Stirling FK8 2E1.)

Lindon, Jennie (2003) *Too Safe for their Own Good? Helping Children Learn about Risk and Life Skills*. London: National Children's Bureau.

Measuring Success: A Guide to Evaluating School Grounds Projects (2004) Learning through Landscapes. (Includes ideas for involving children of all ages in the evaluation of their grounds. Some of the ideas appropriate to children under five have been included in this publication.)

Ouvry, Marjorie (2003) *Exercising Muscles and Minds: Outdoor Play and the Early Years Curriculum*. London: NCB Books.

Rich, Diane (2004) *Listening to Babies*. Listening as a Way of Life series. London: National Children's Bureau.

Tickell, Clare (2011) *The Early Years: Foundations for Life, Health and Learning*. London: DfEE. www.education.gov.uk/tickellreview